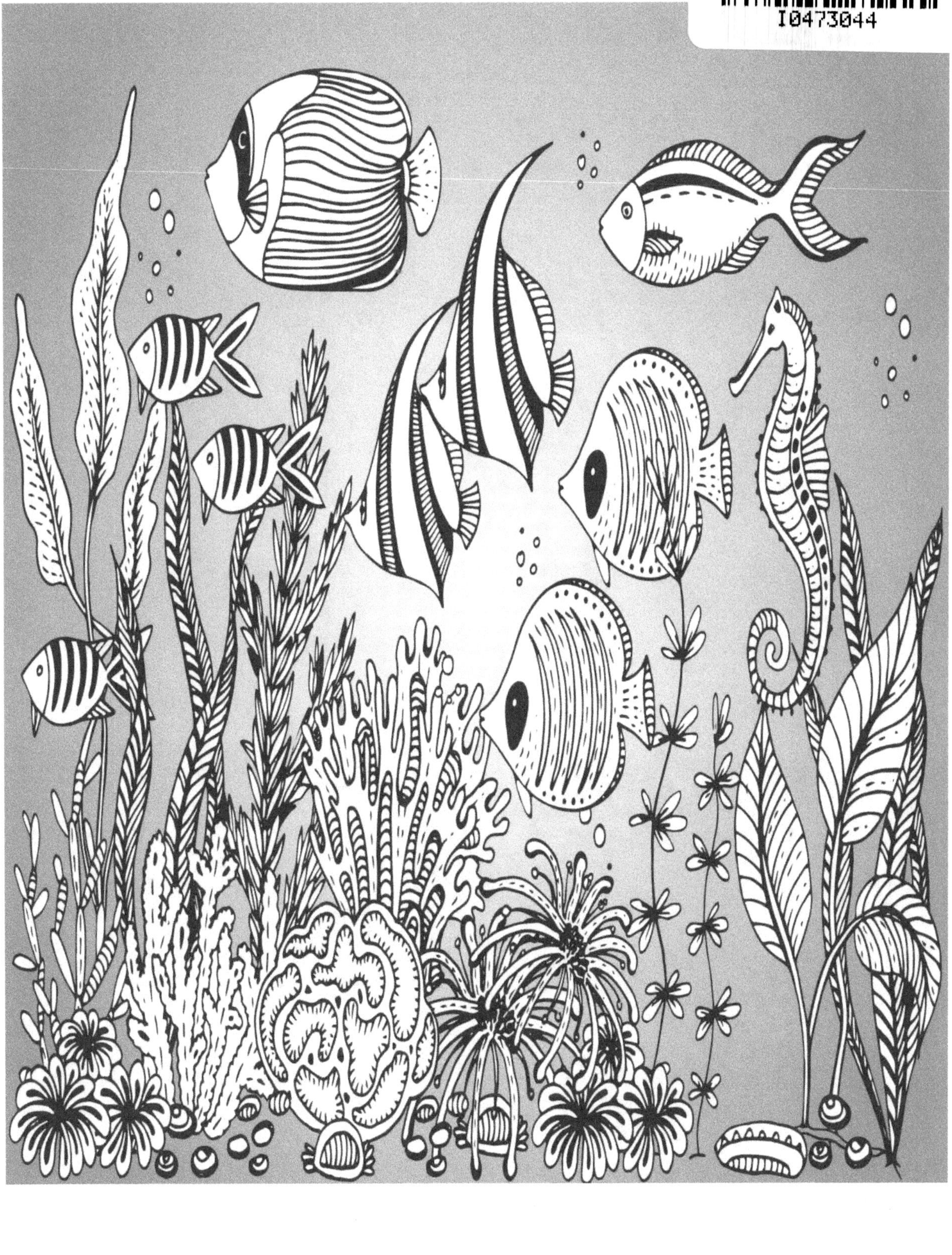

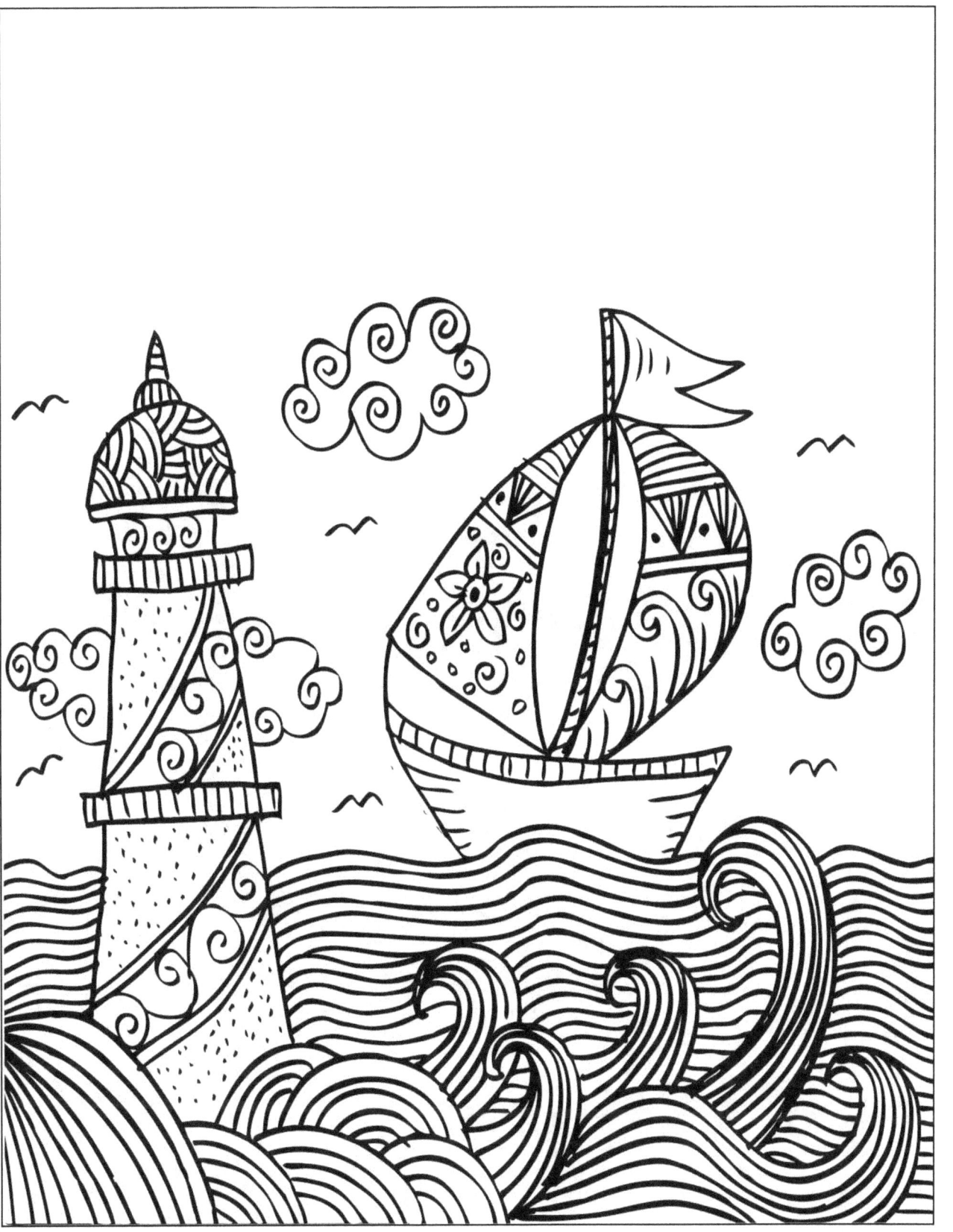

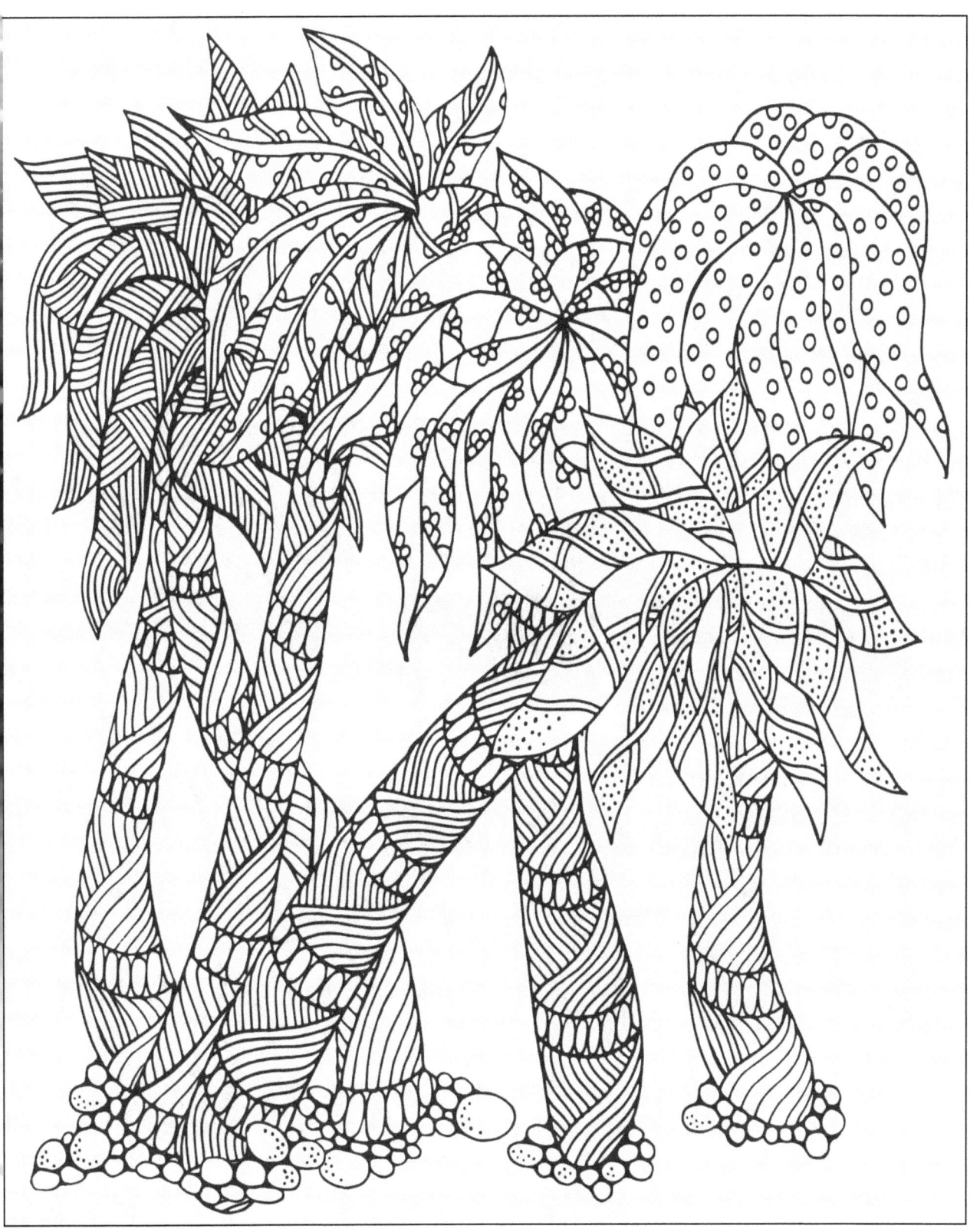

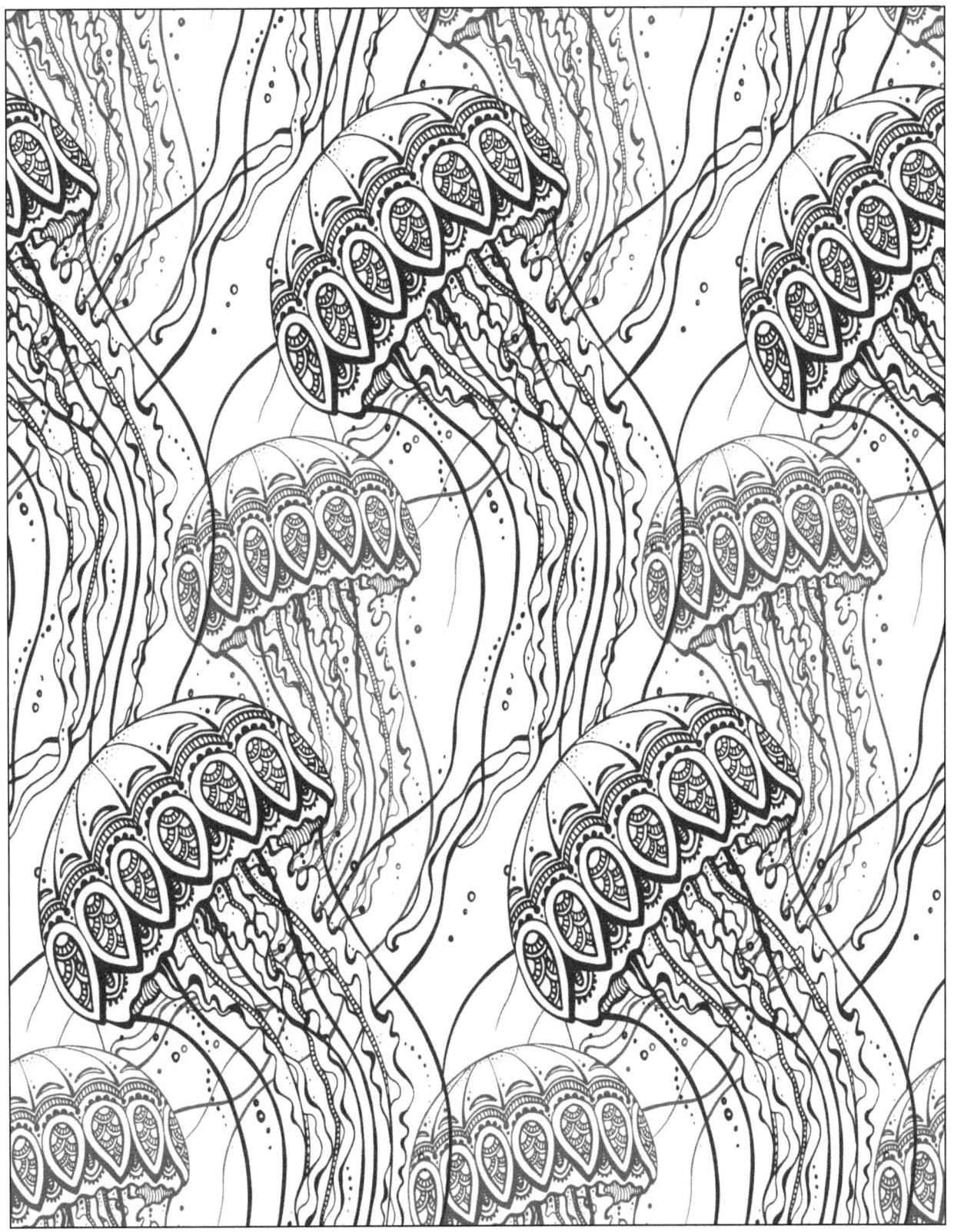

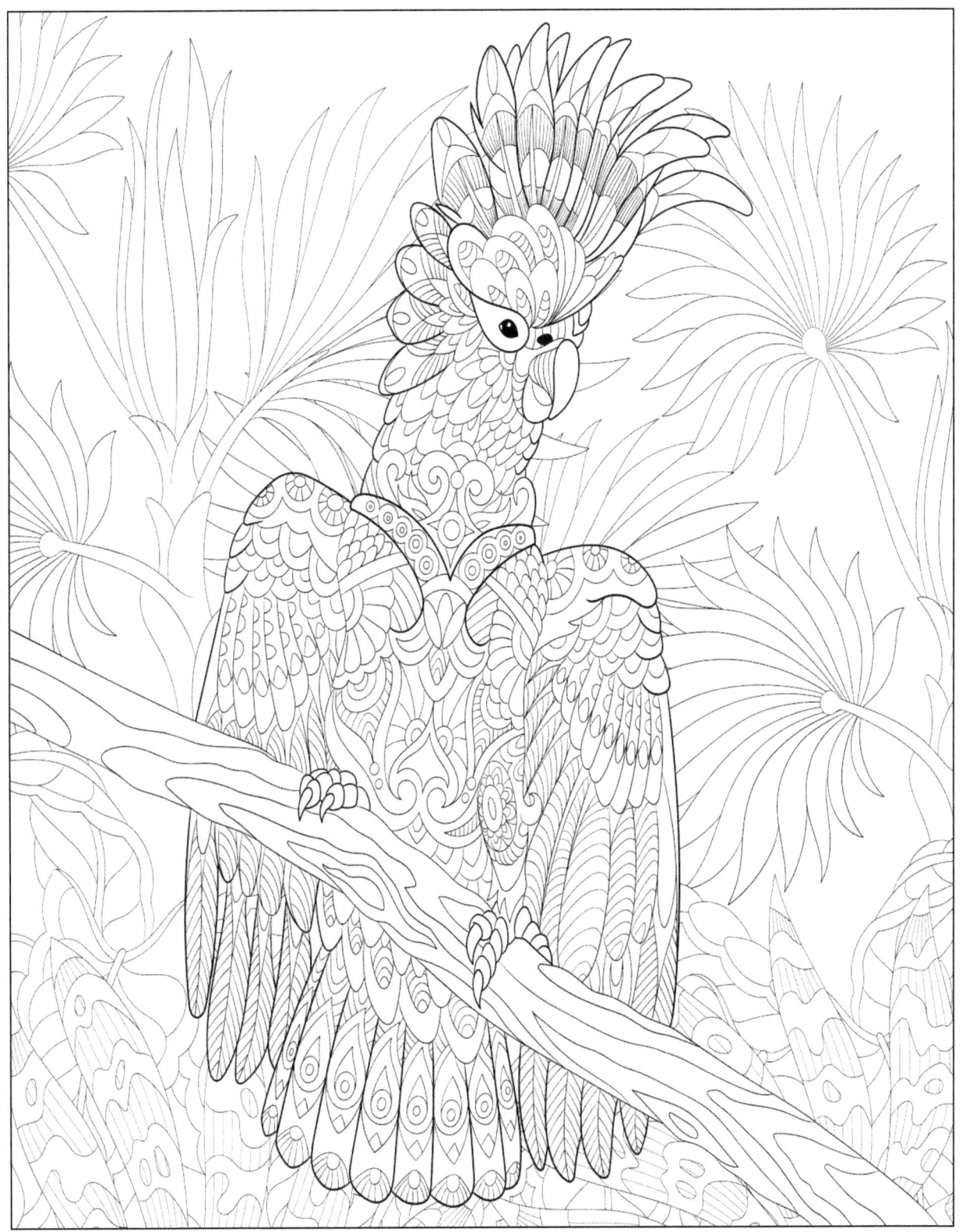

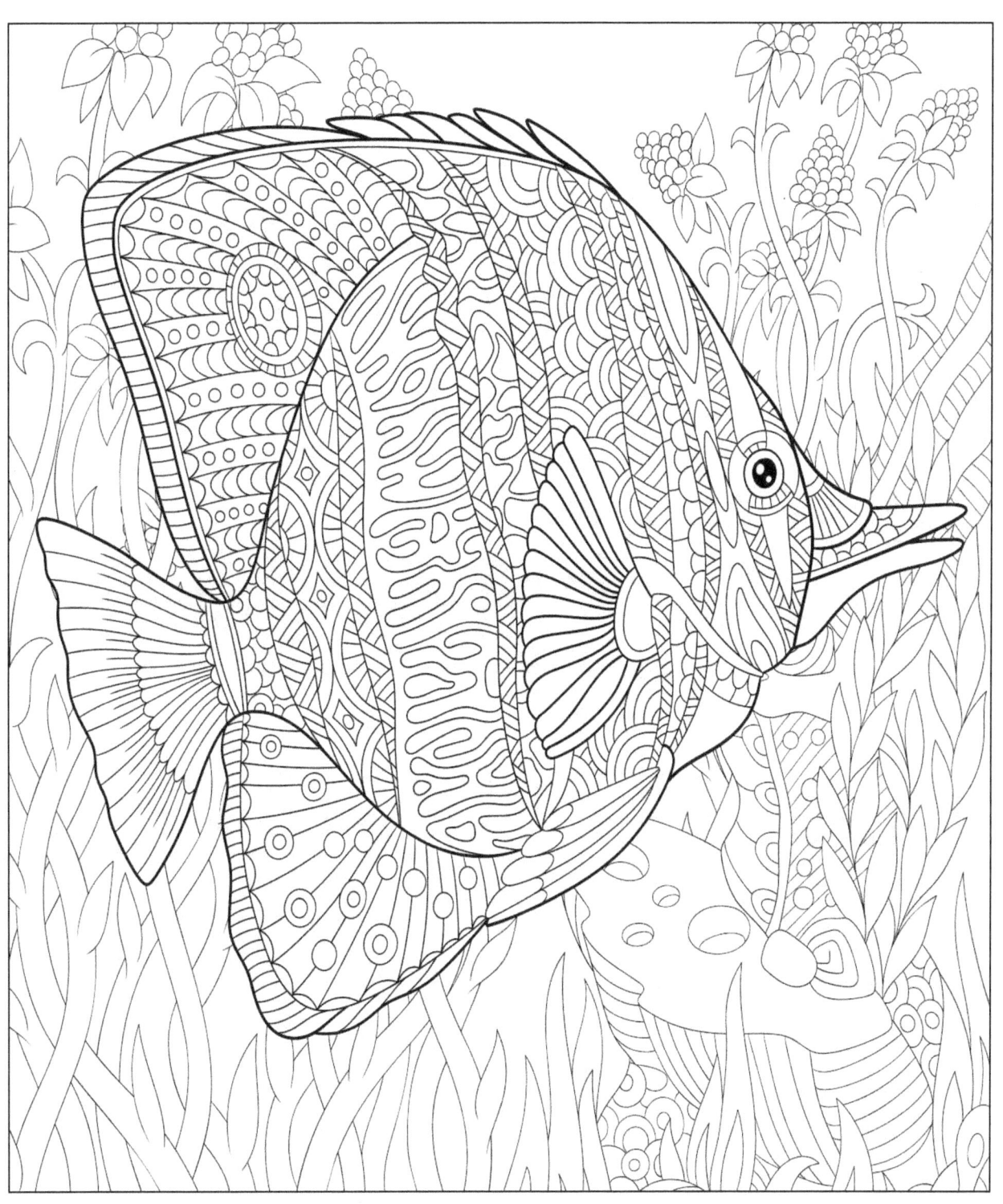

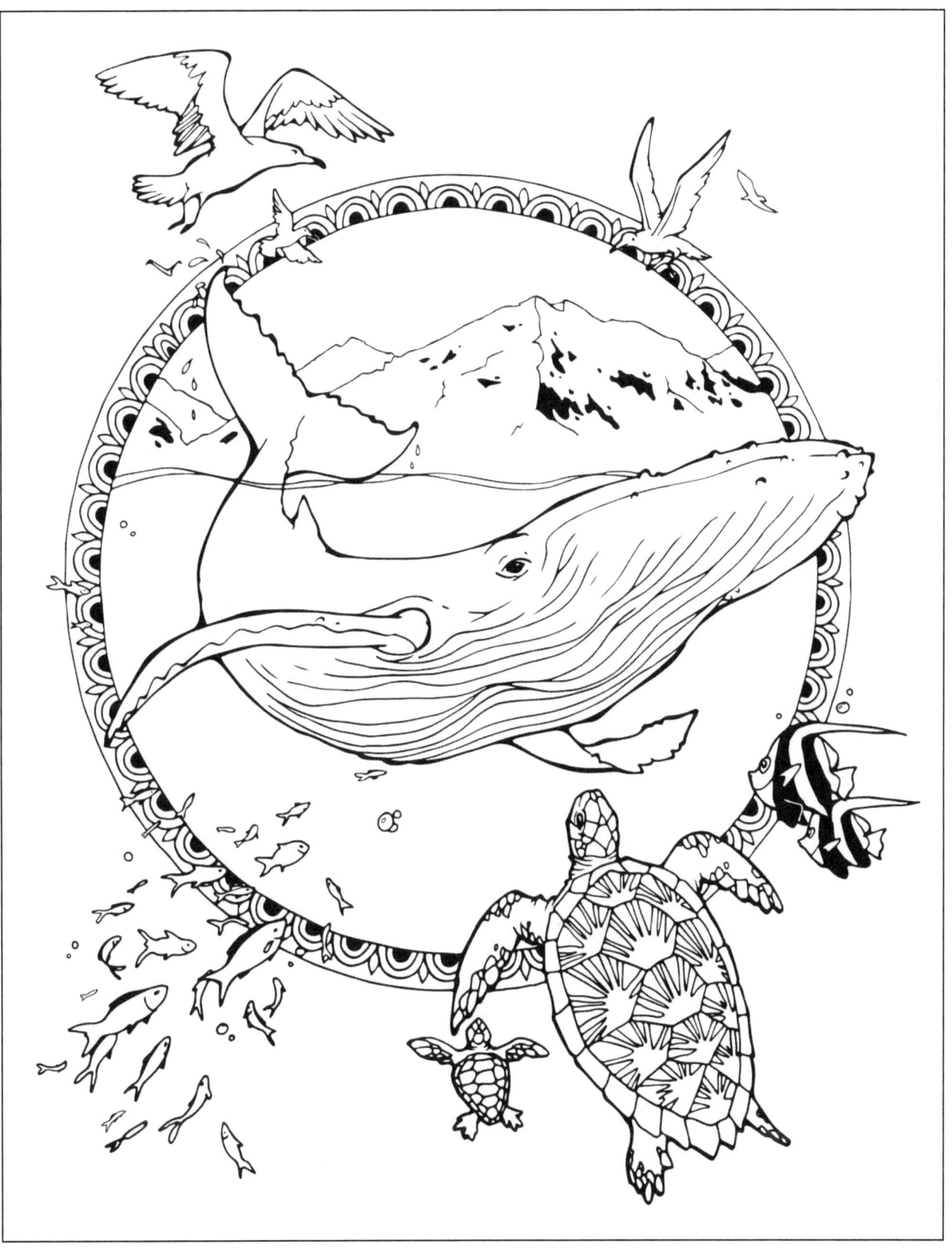

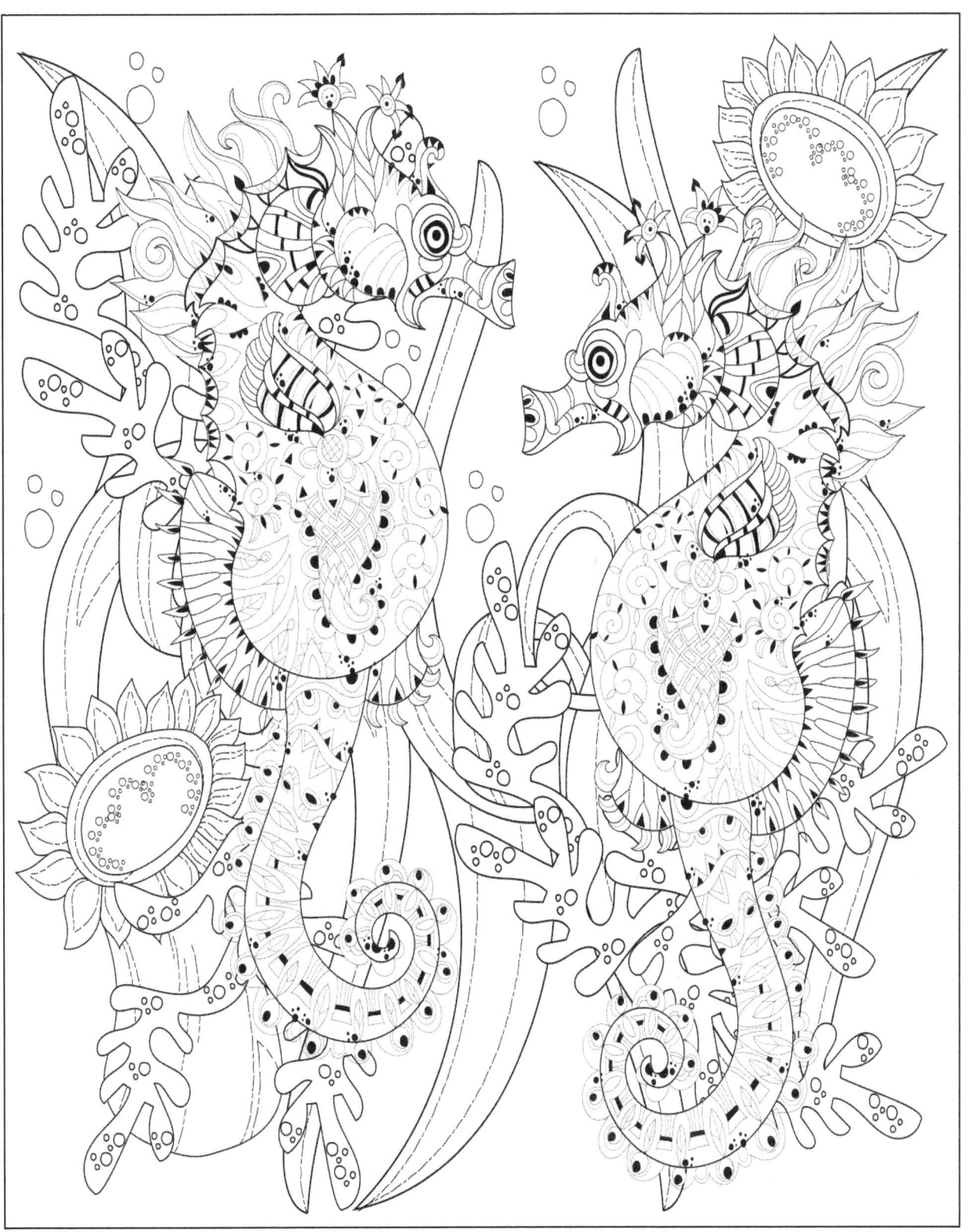

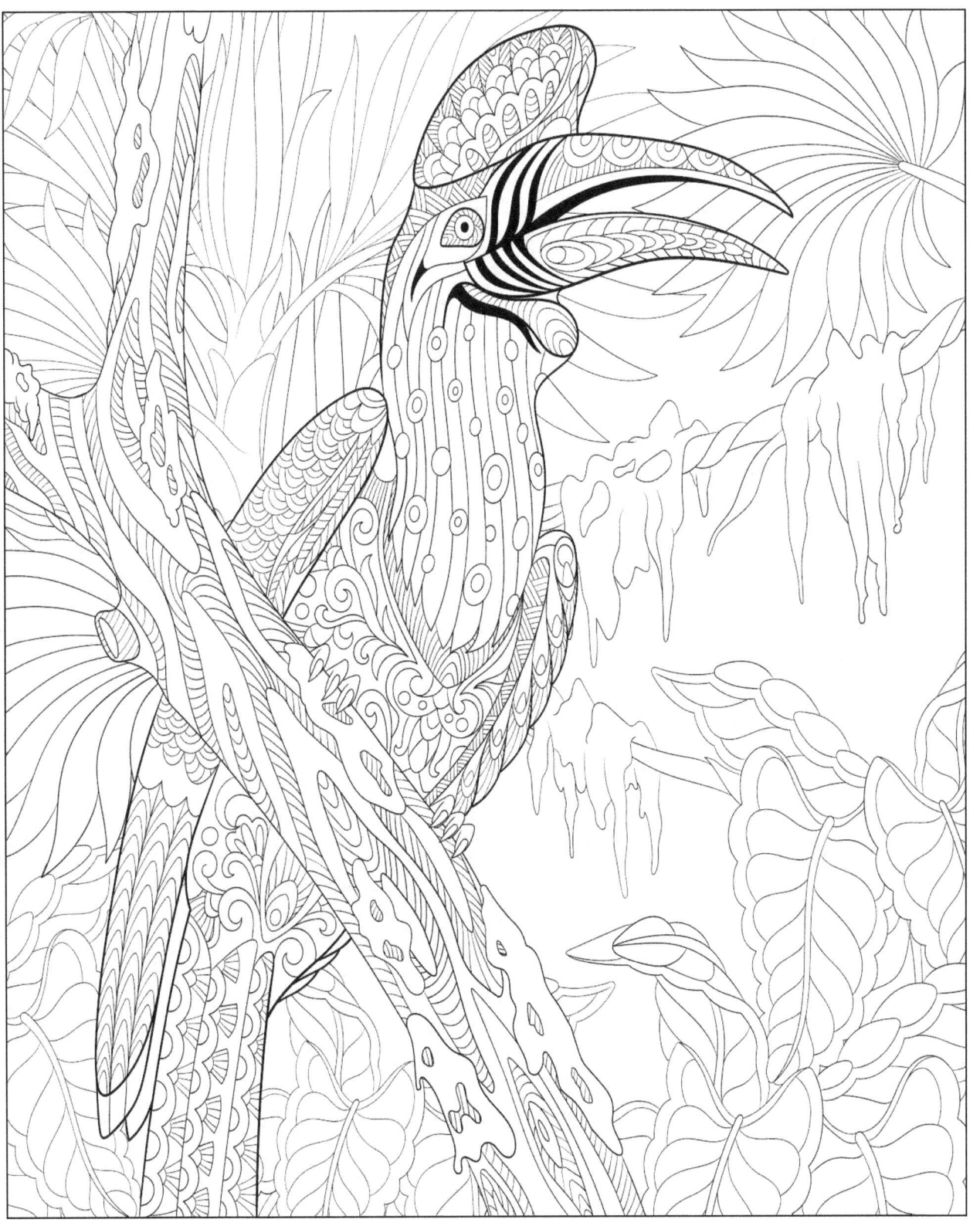

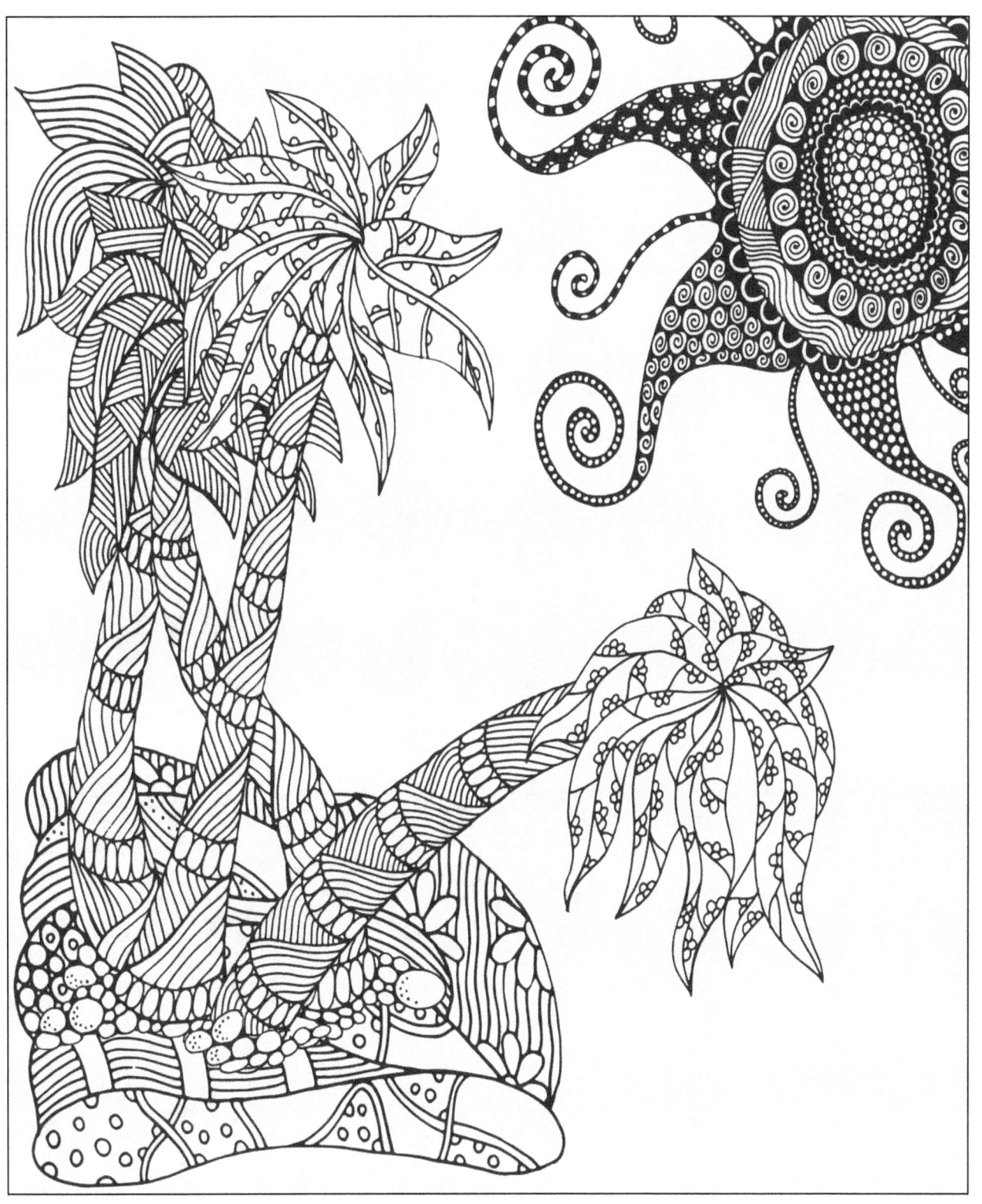

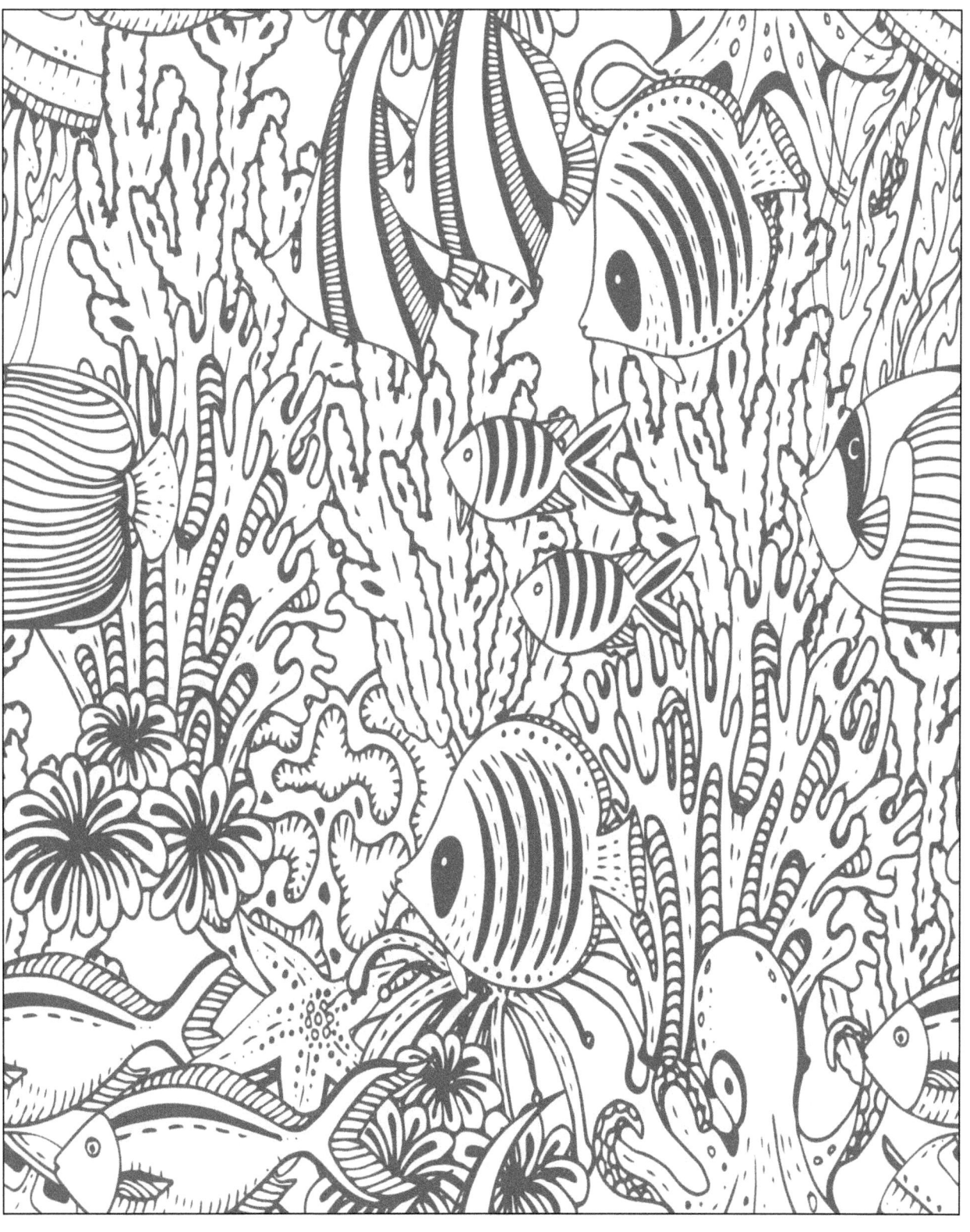

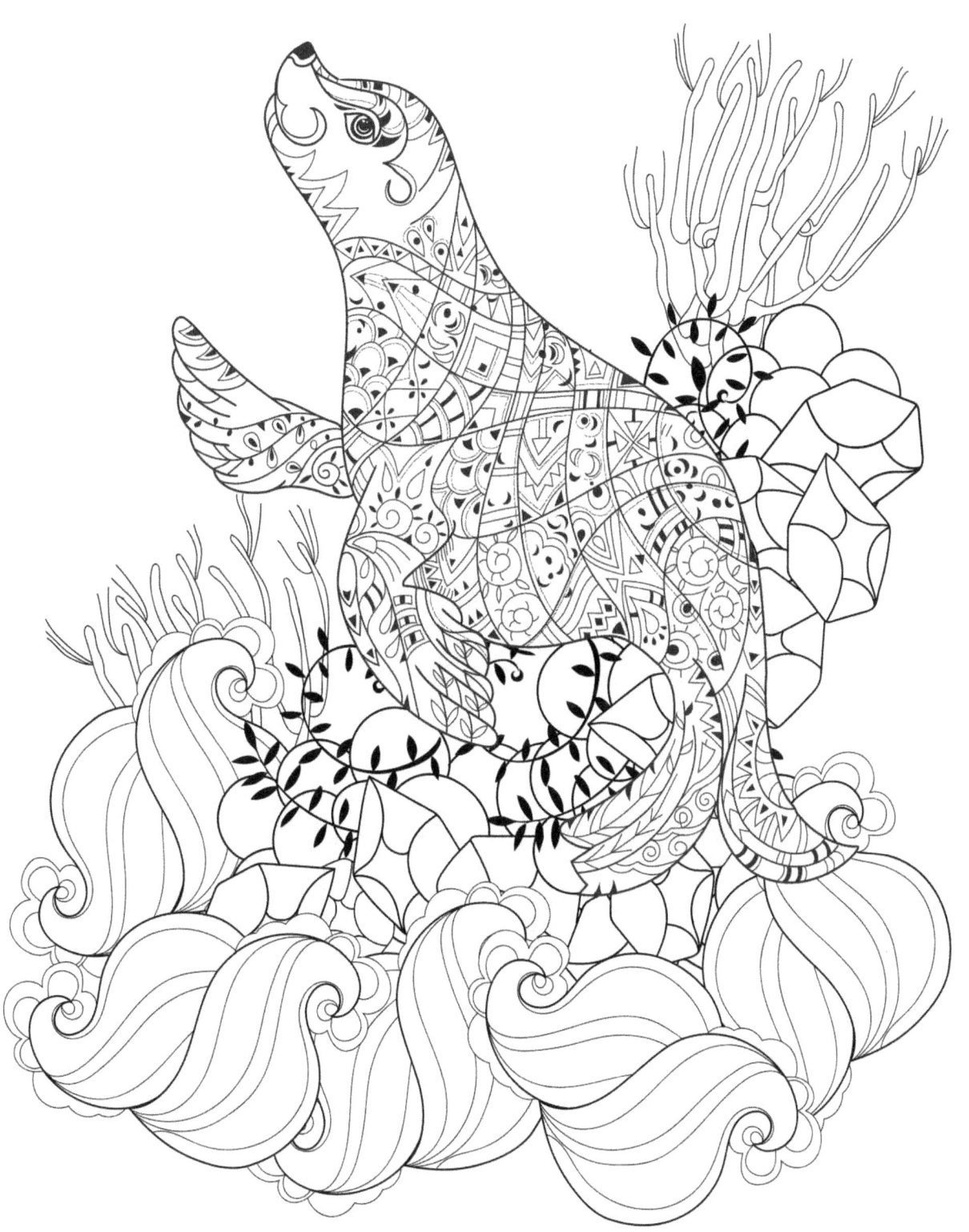

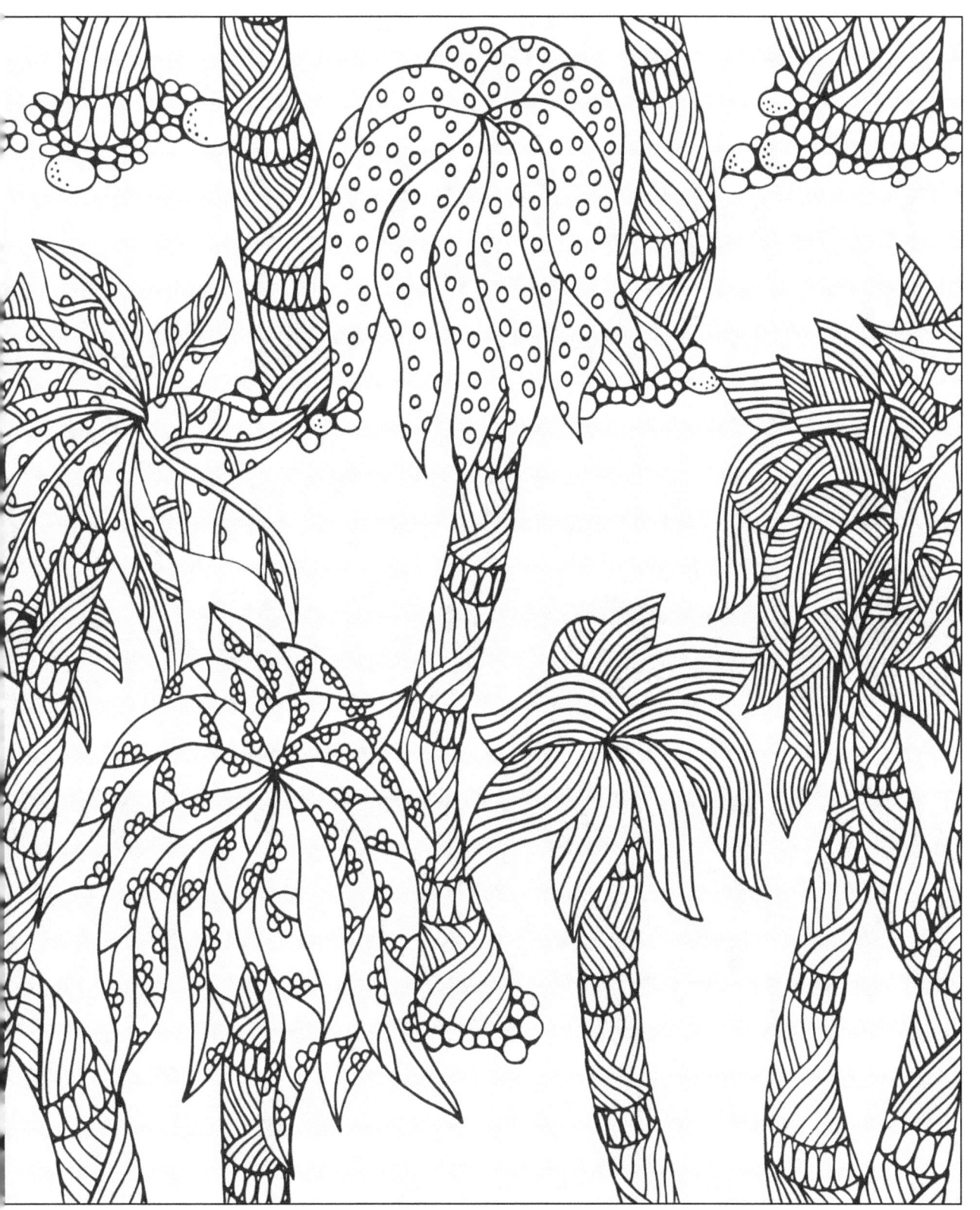

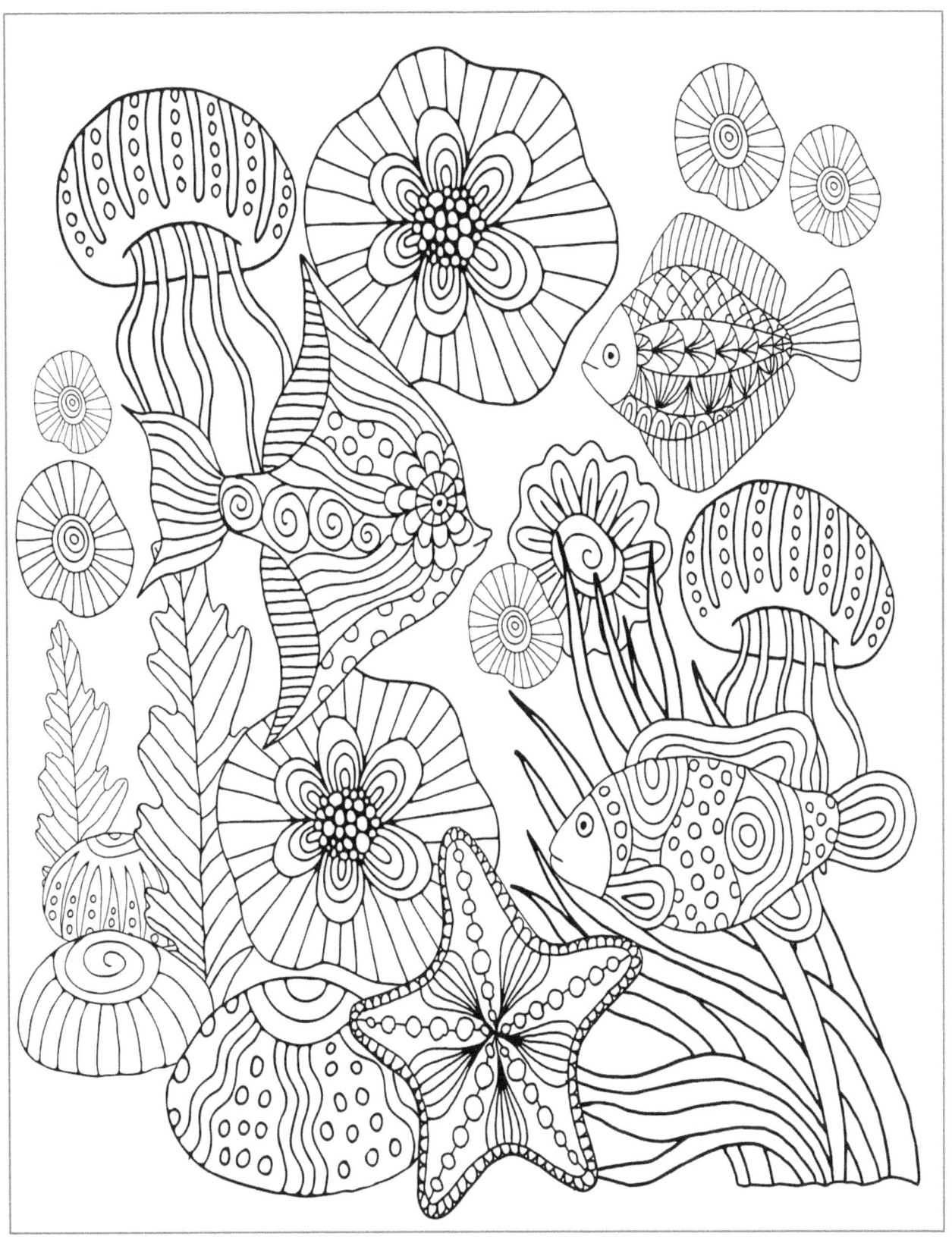

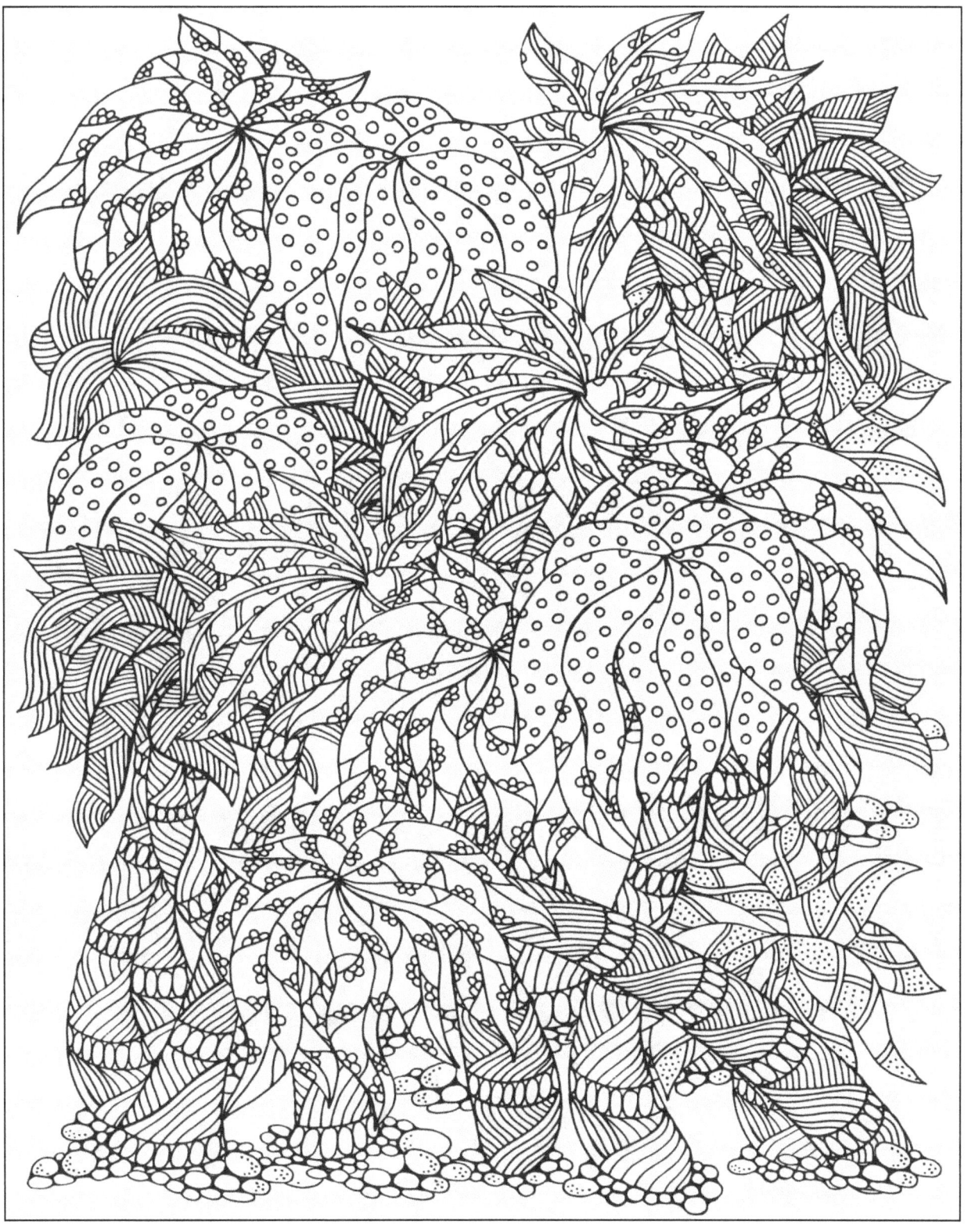

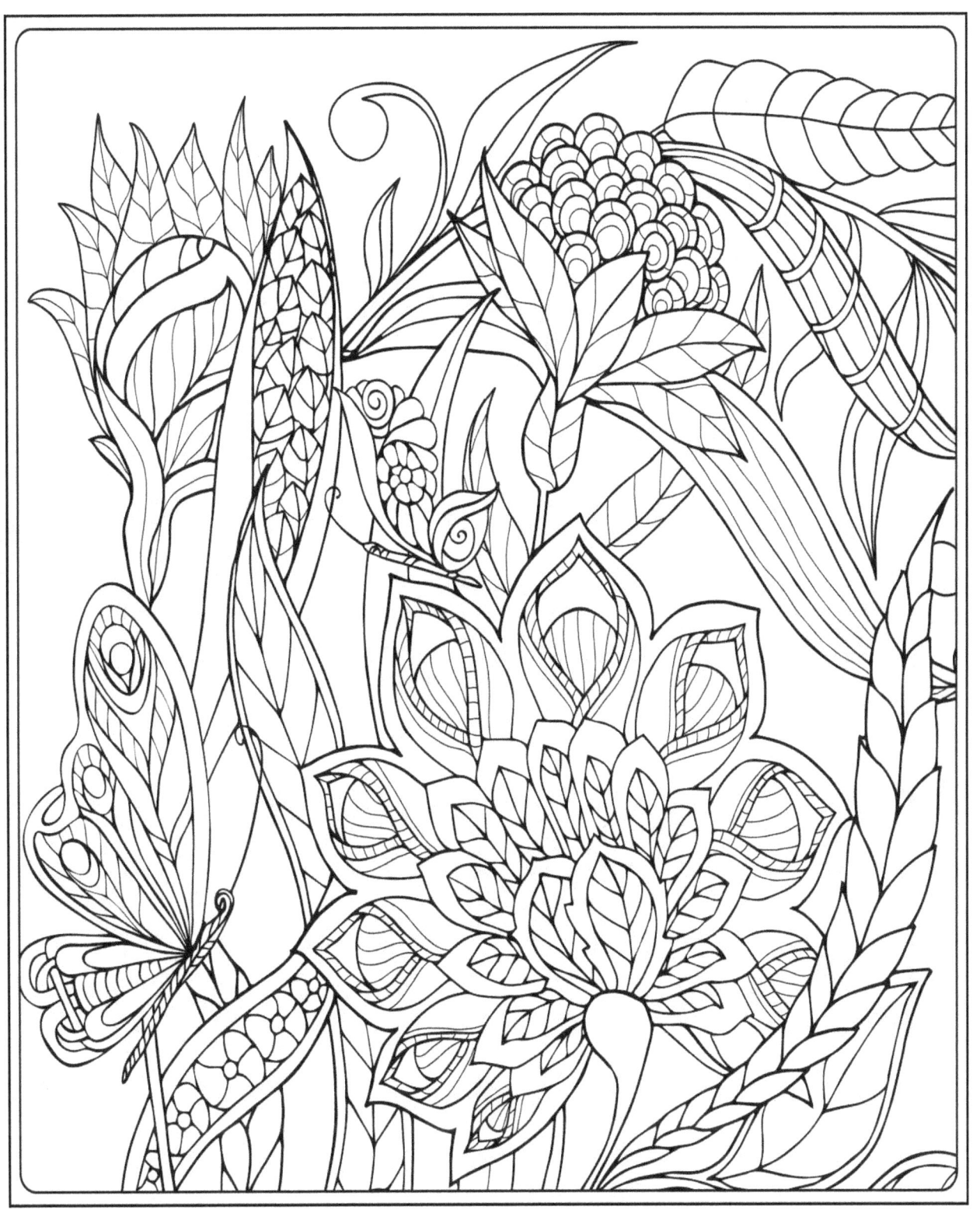

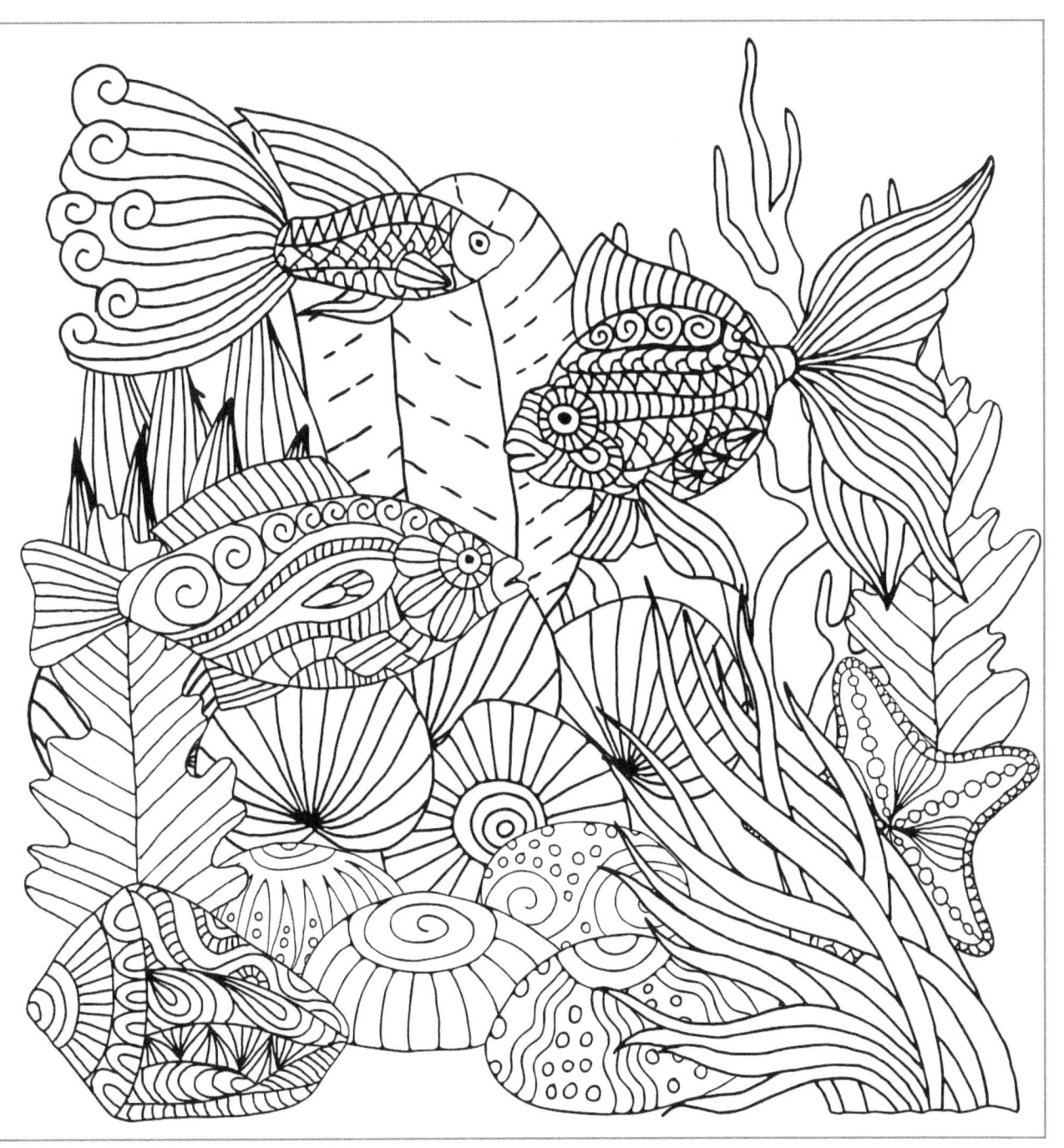

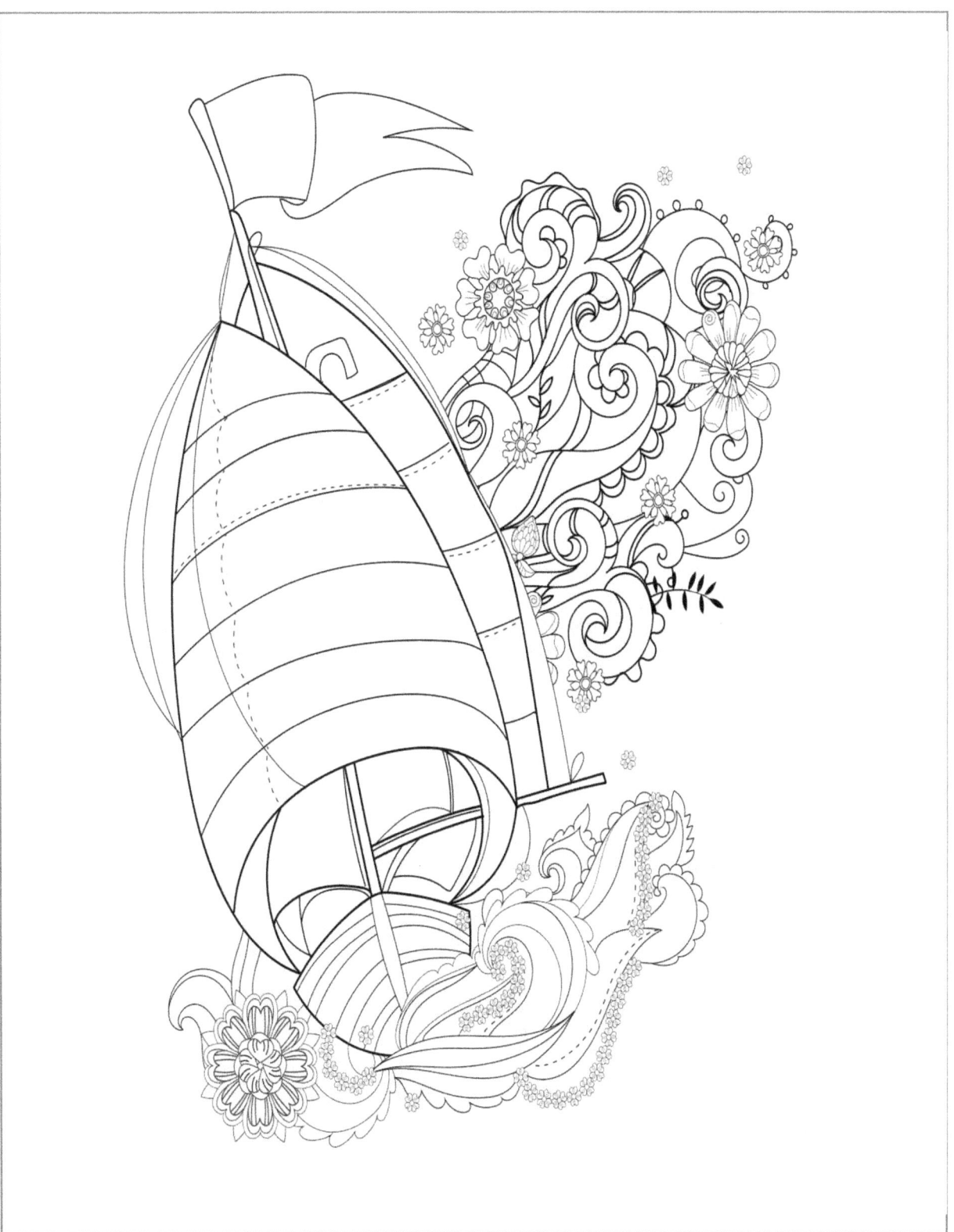

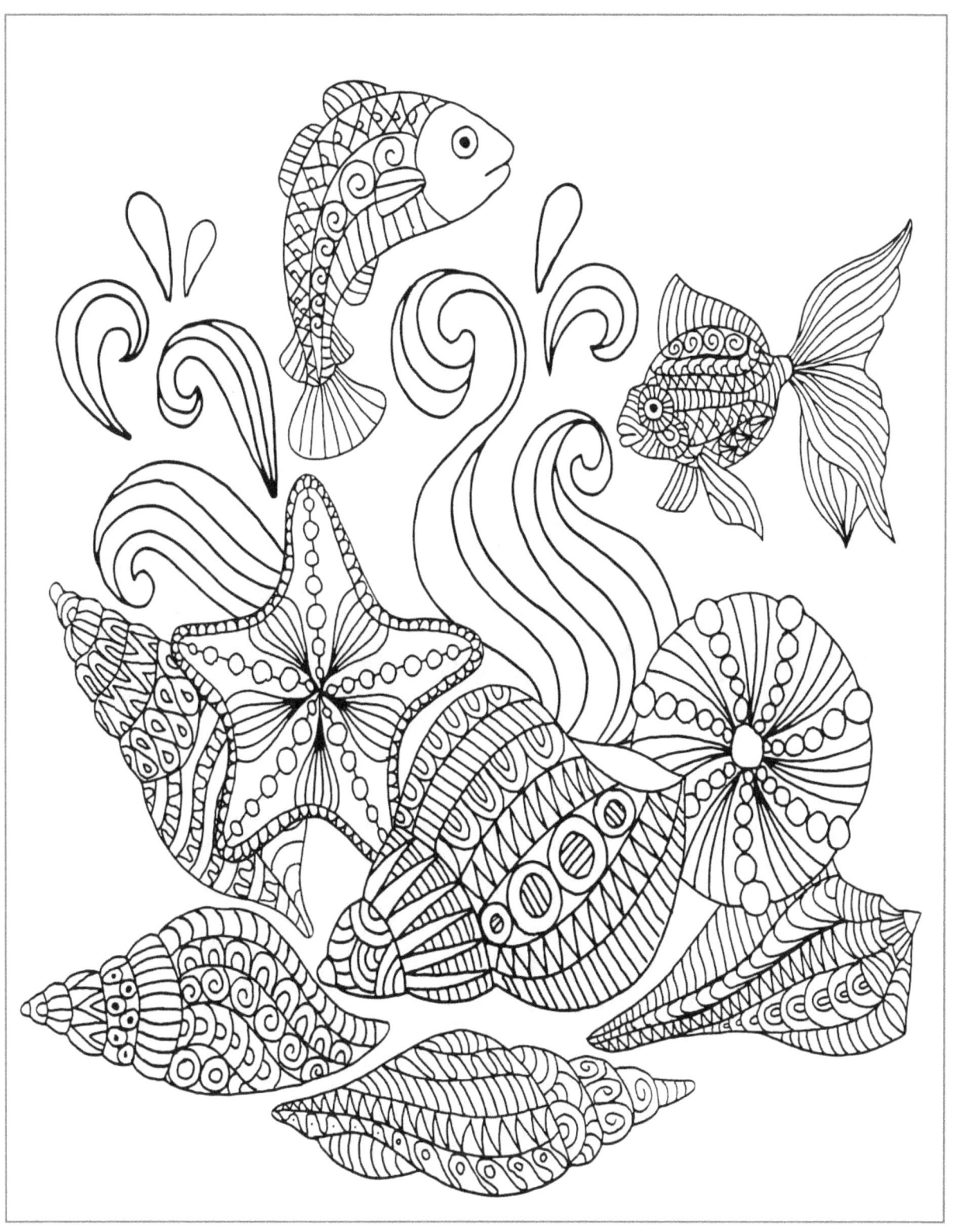

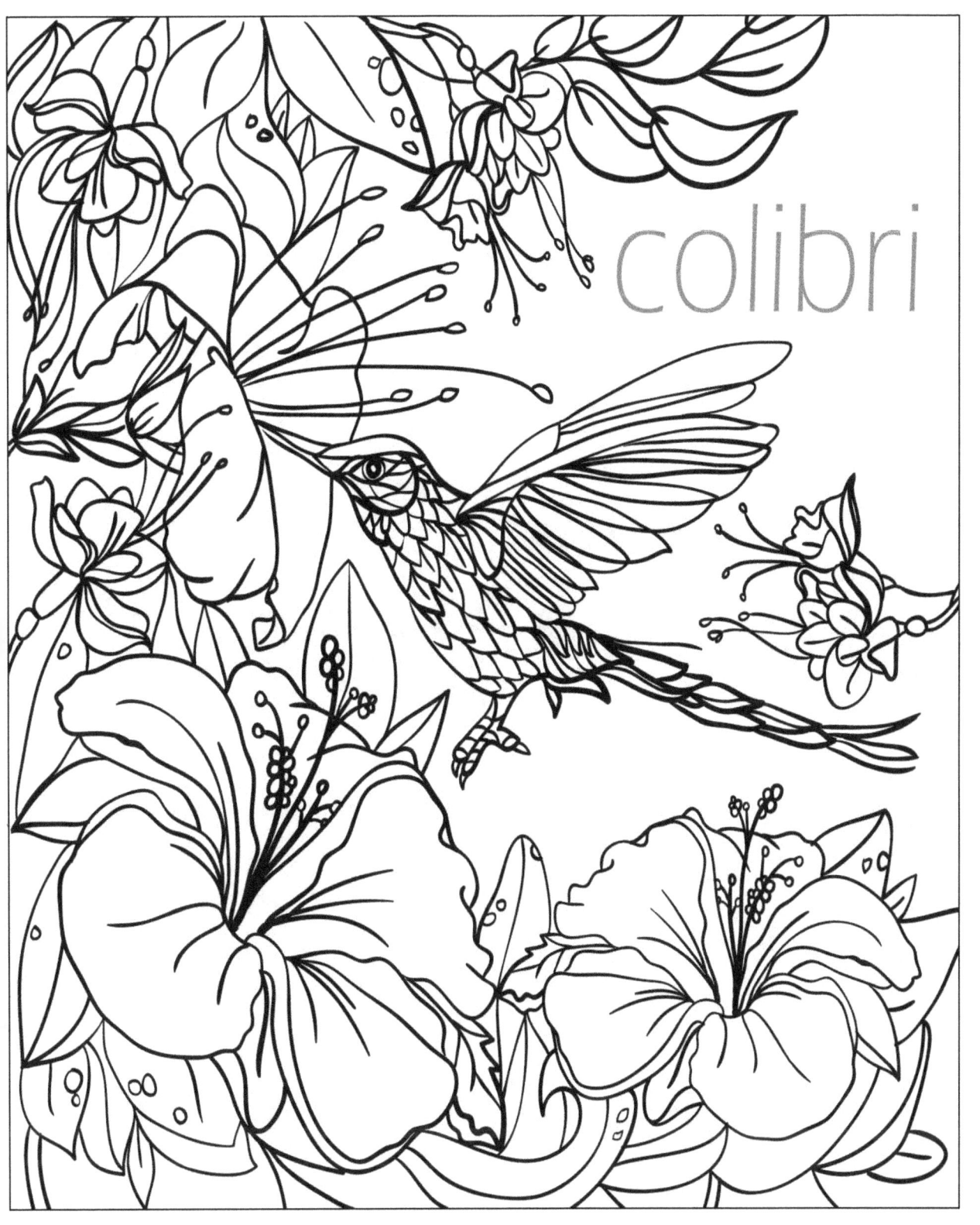
colibri

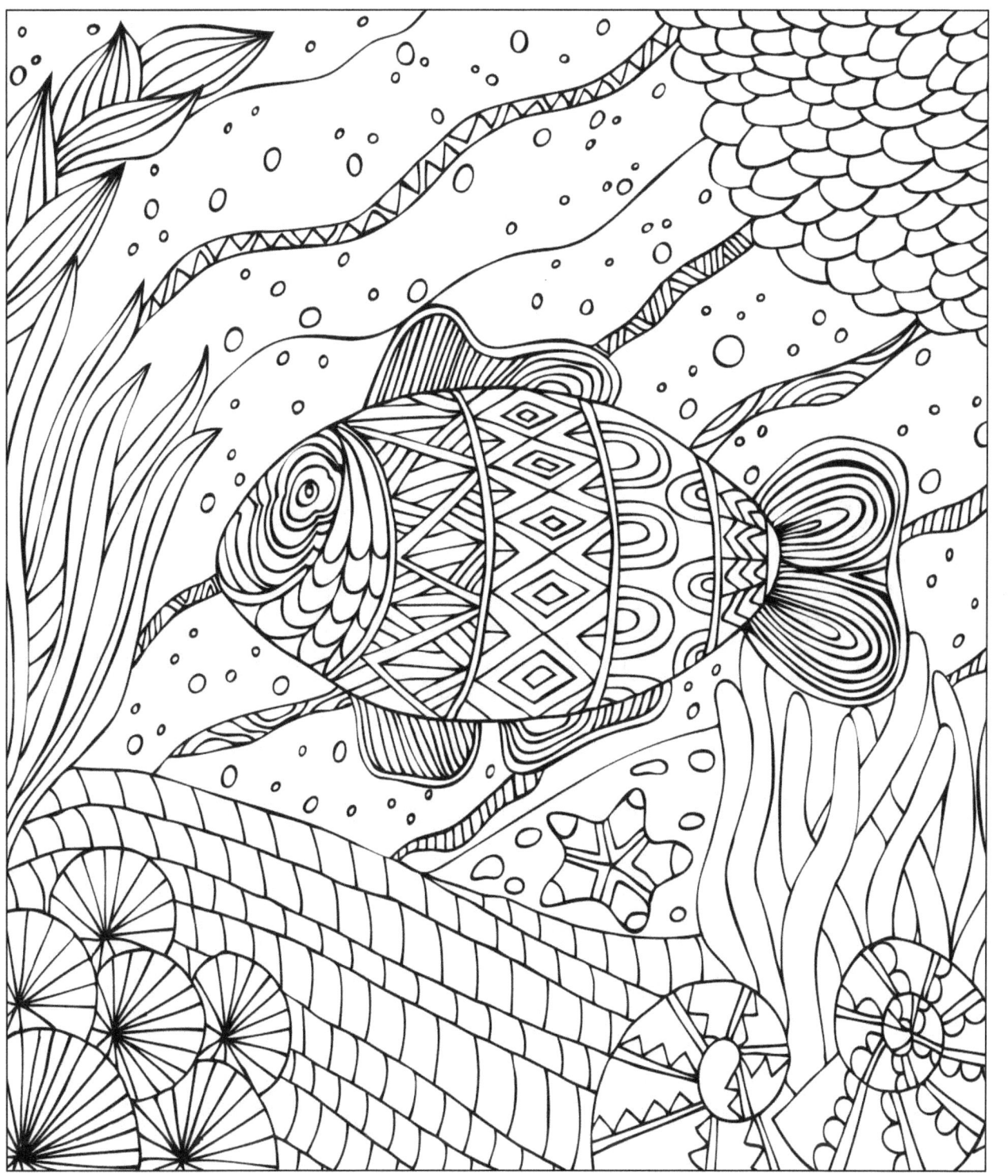

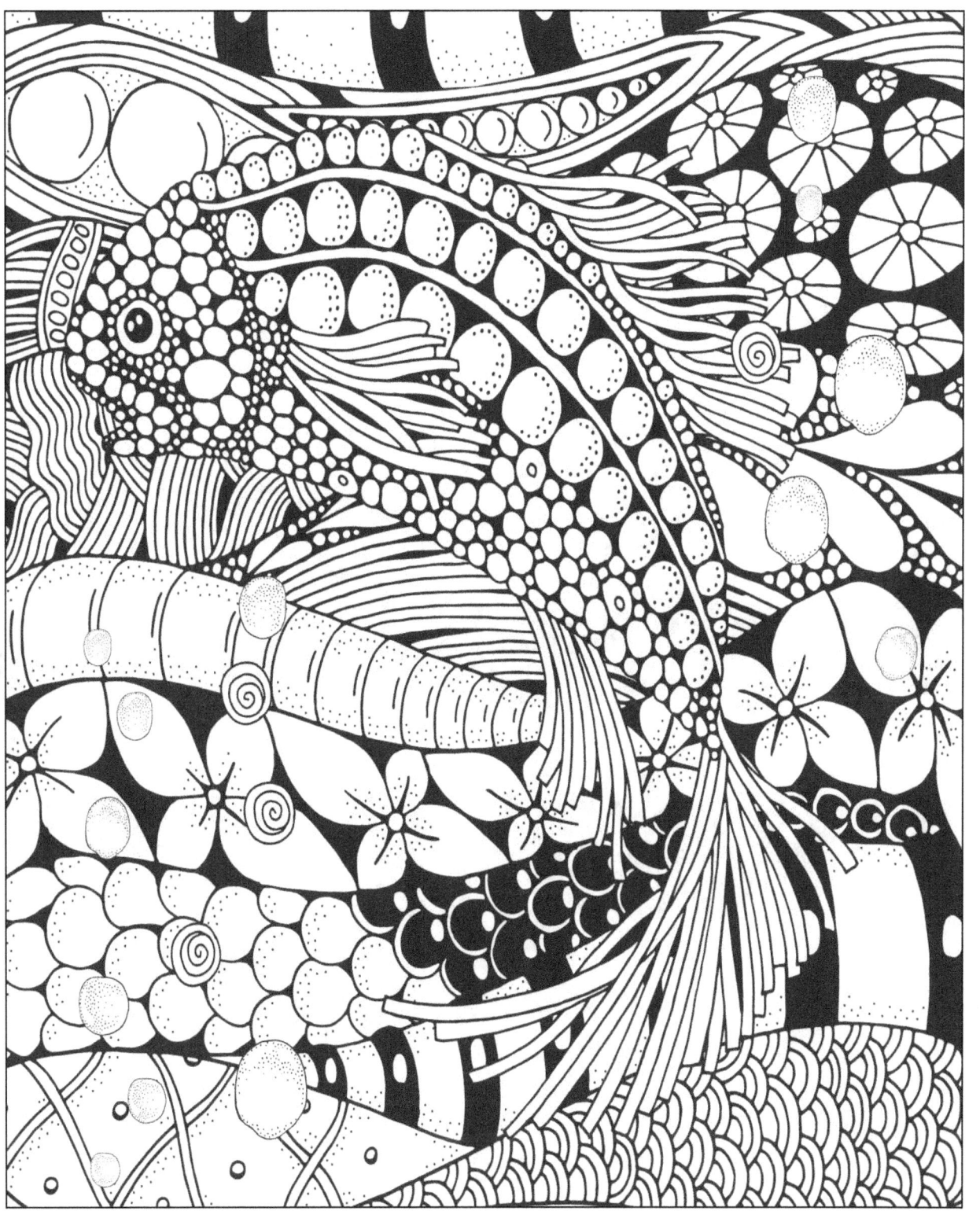

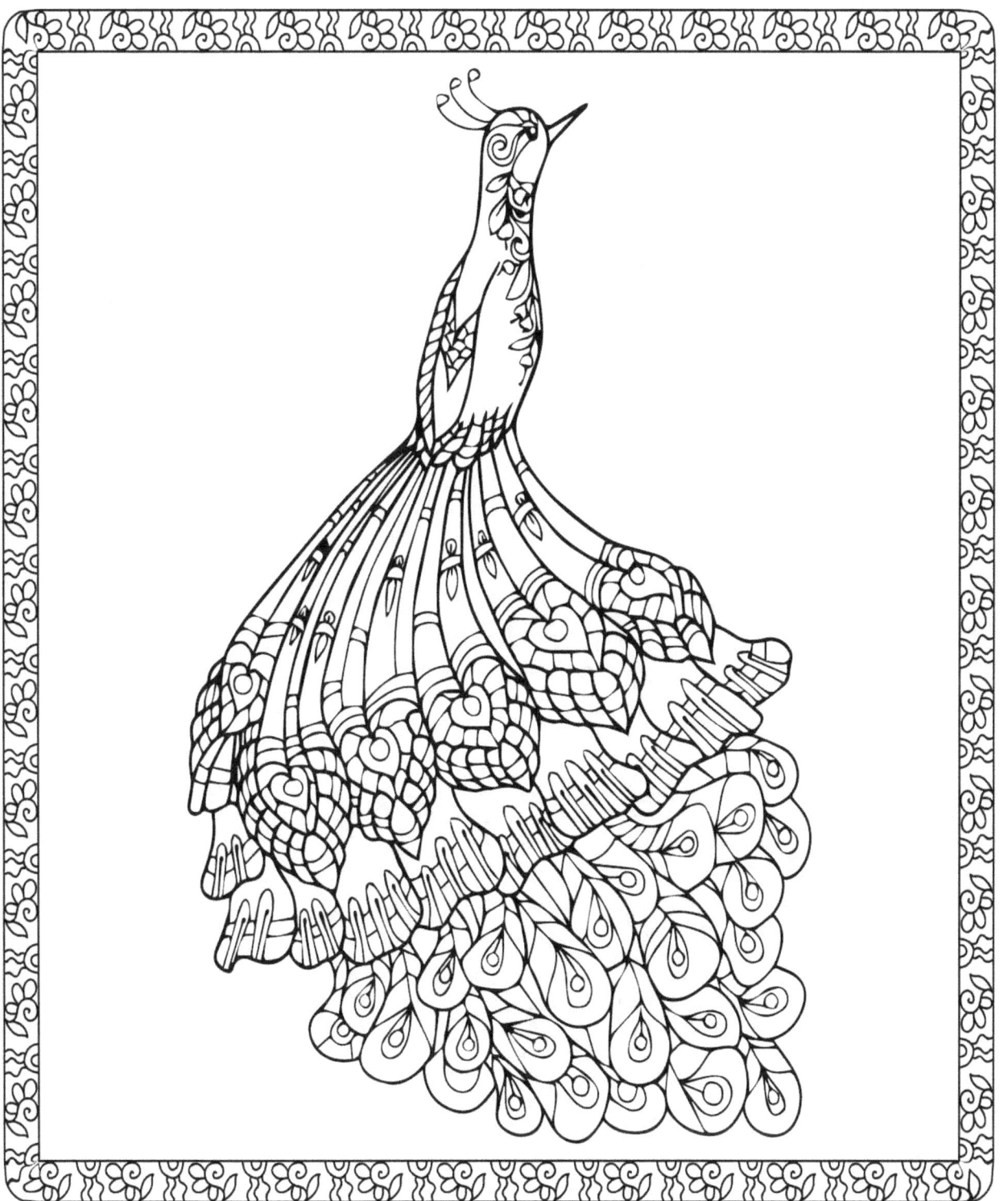

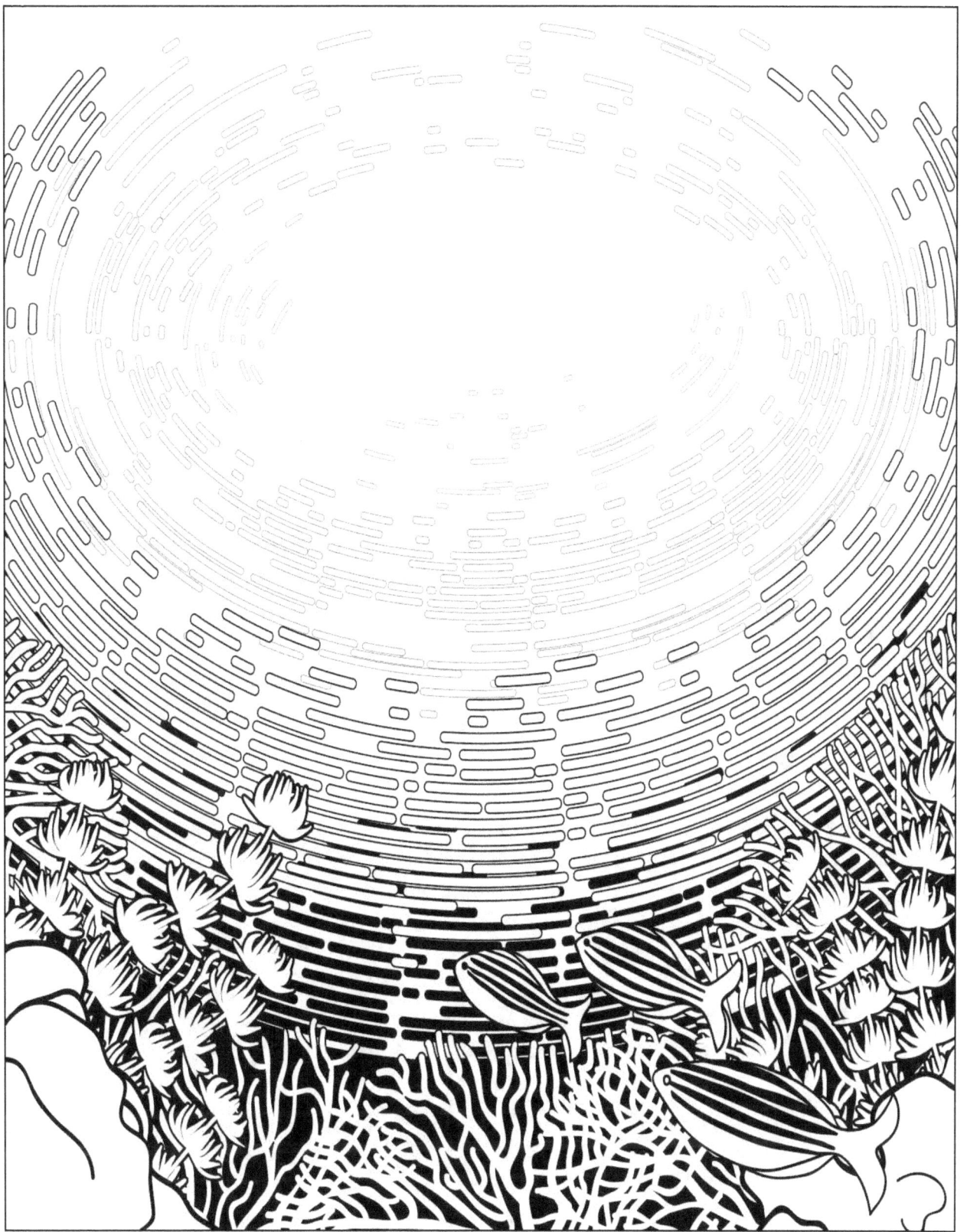

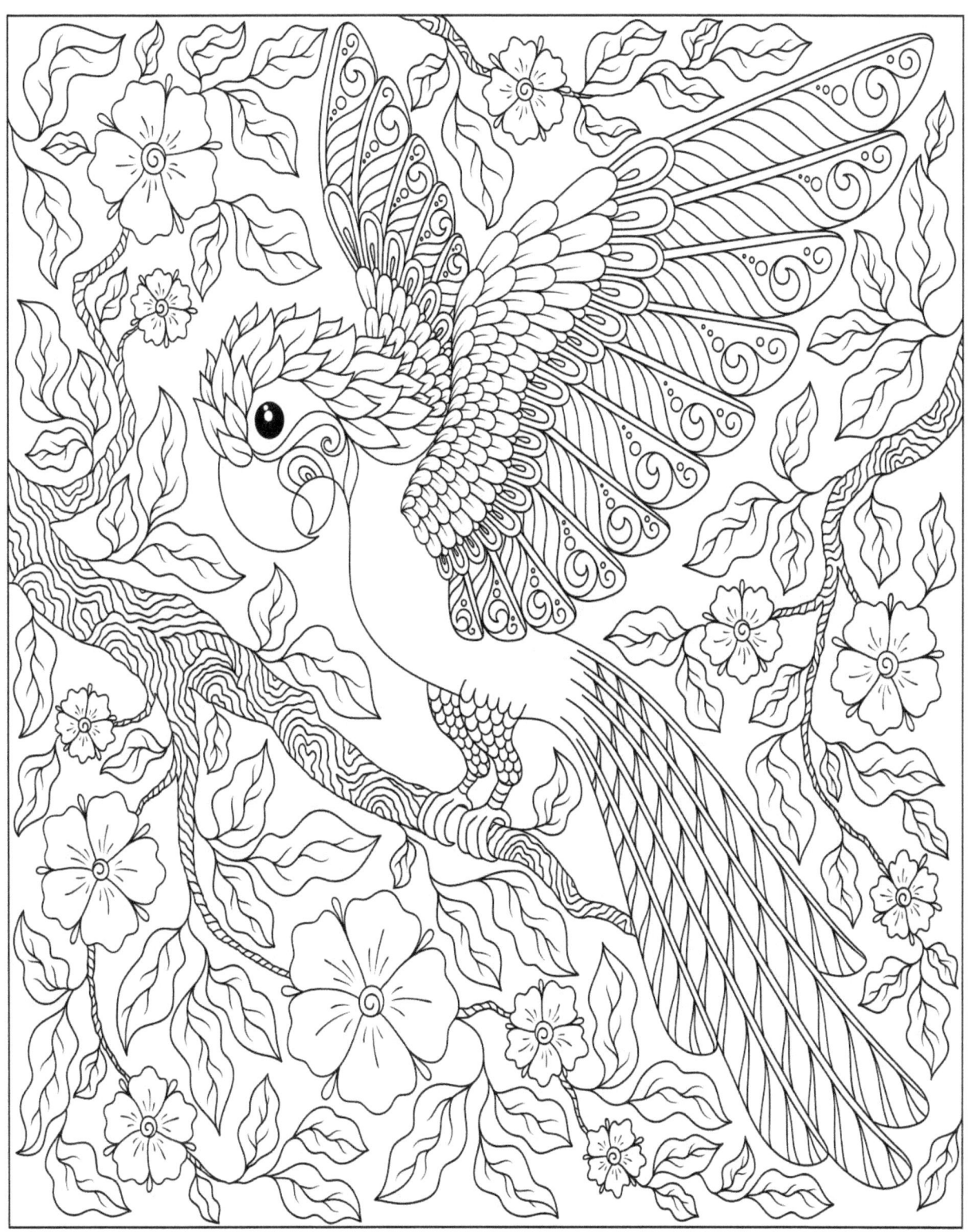

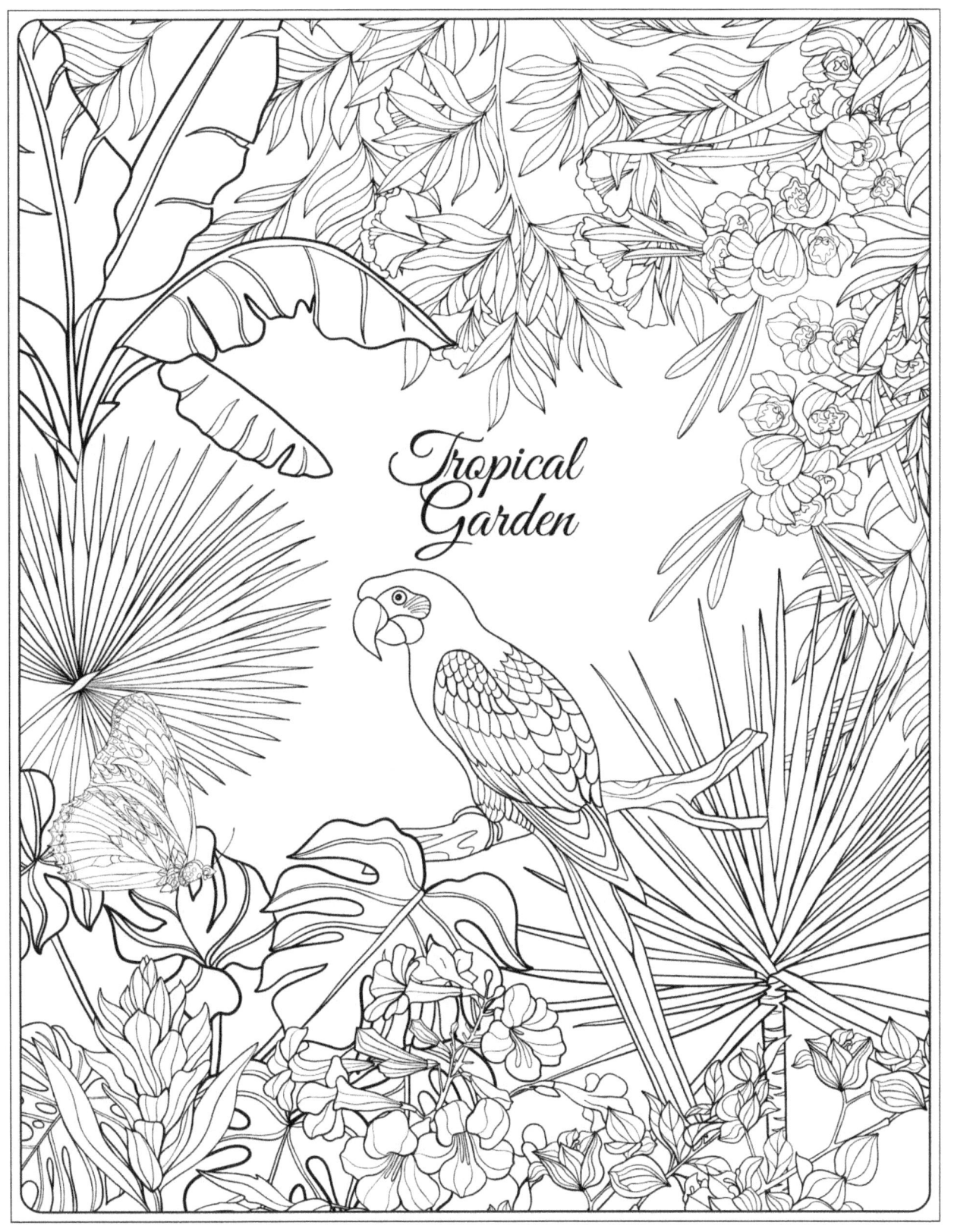

Tropical
Garden

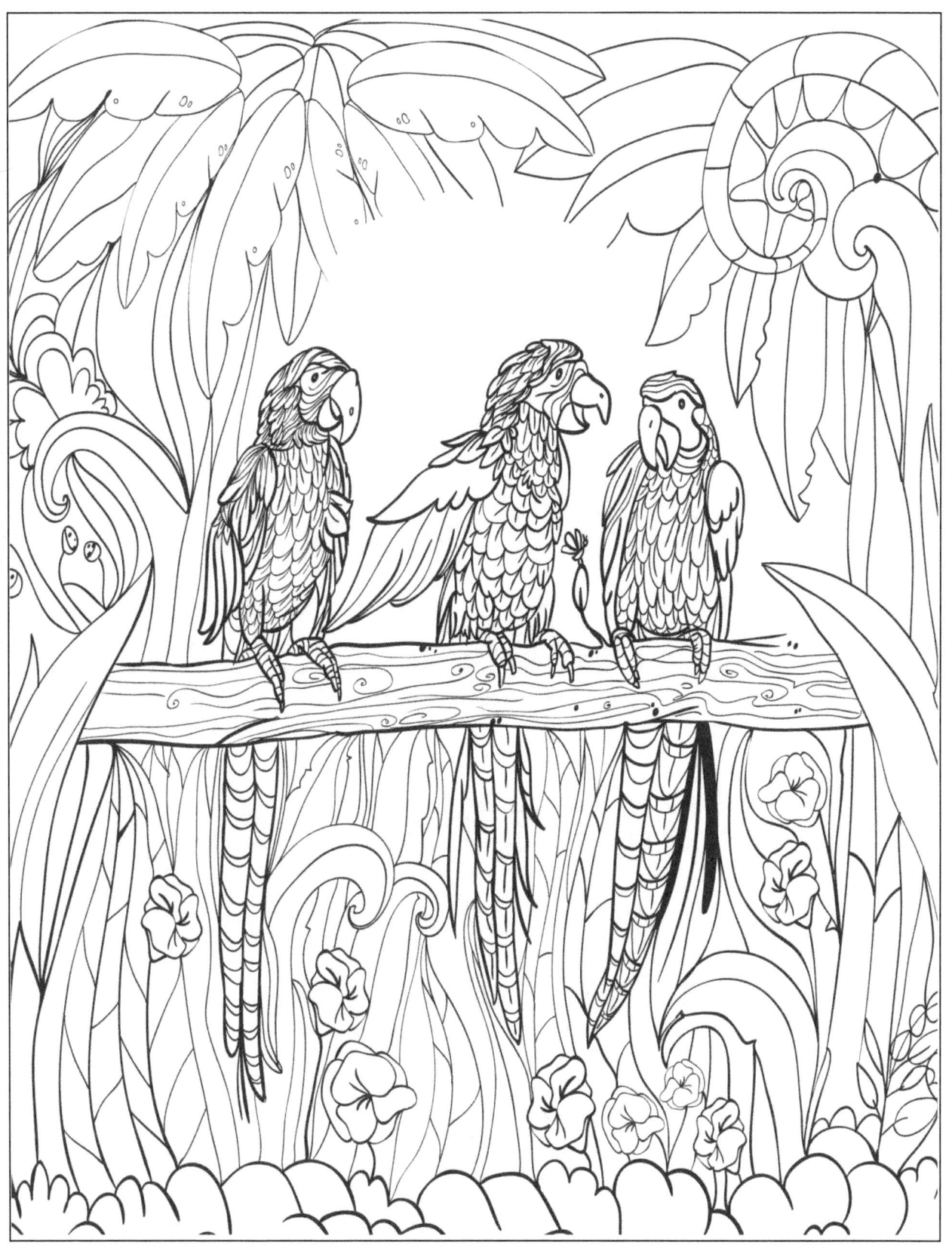

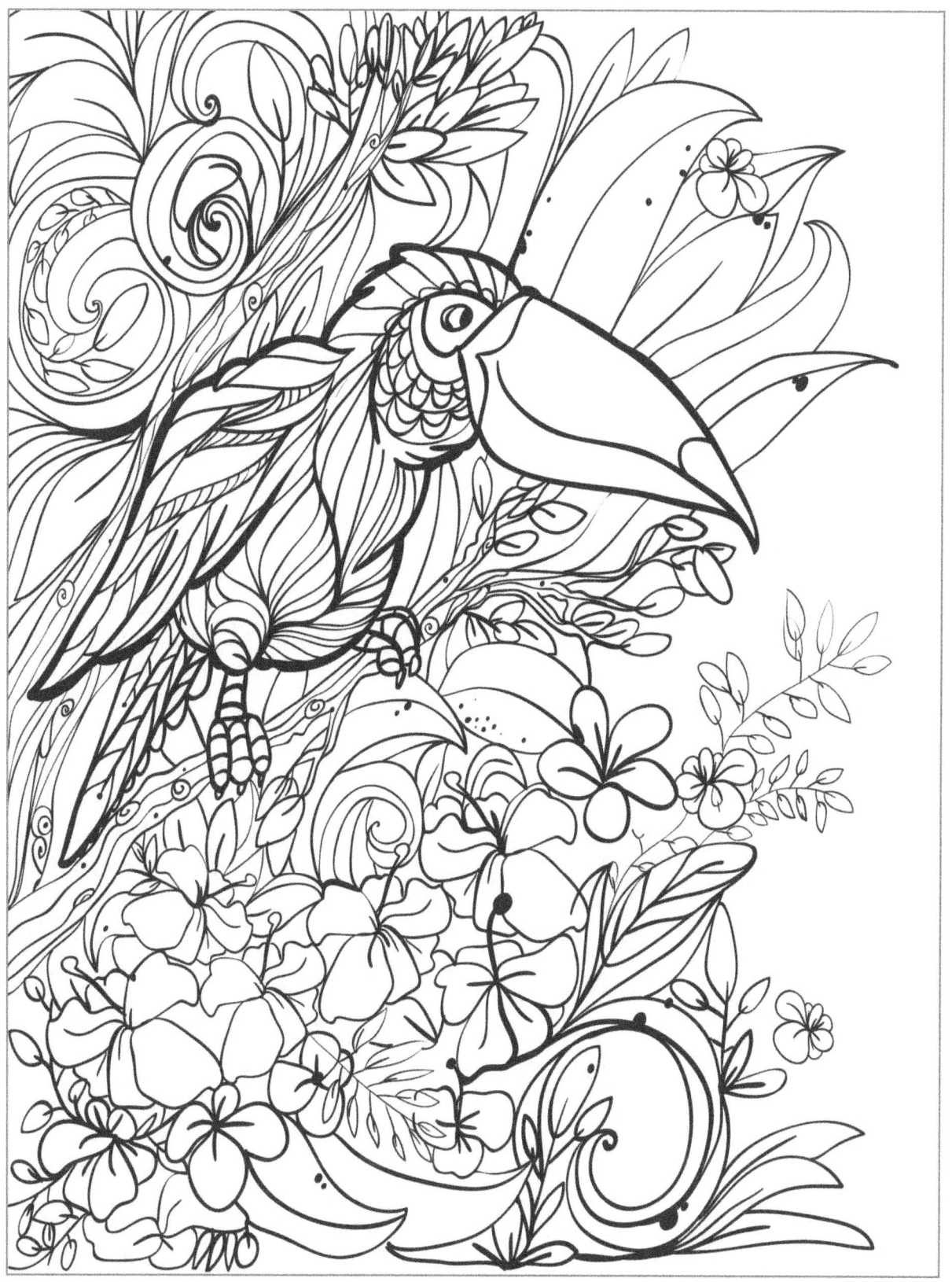

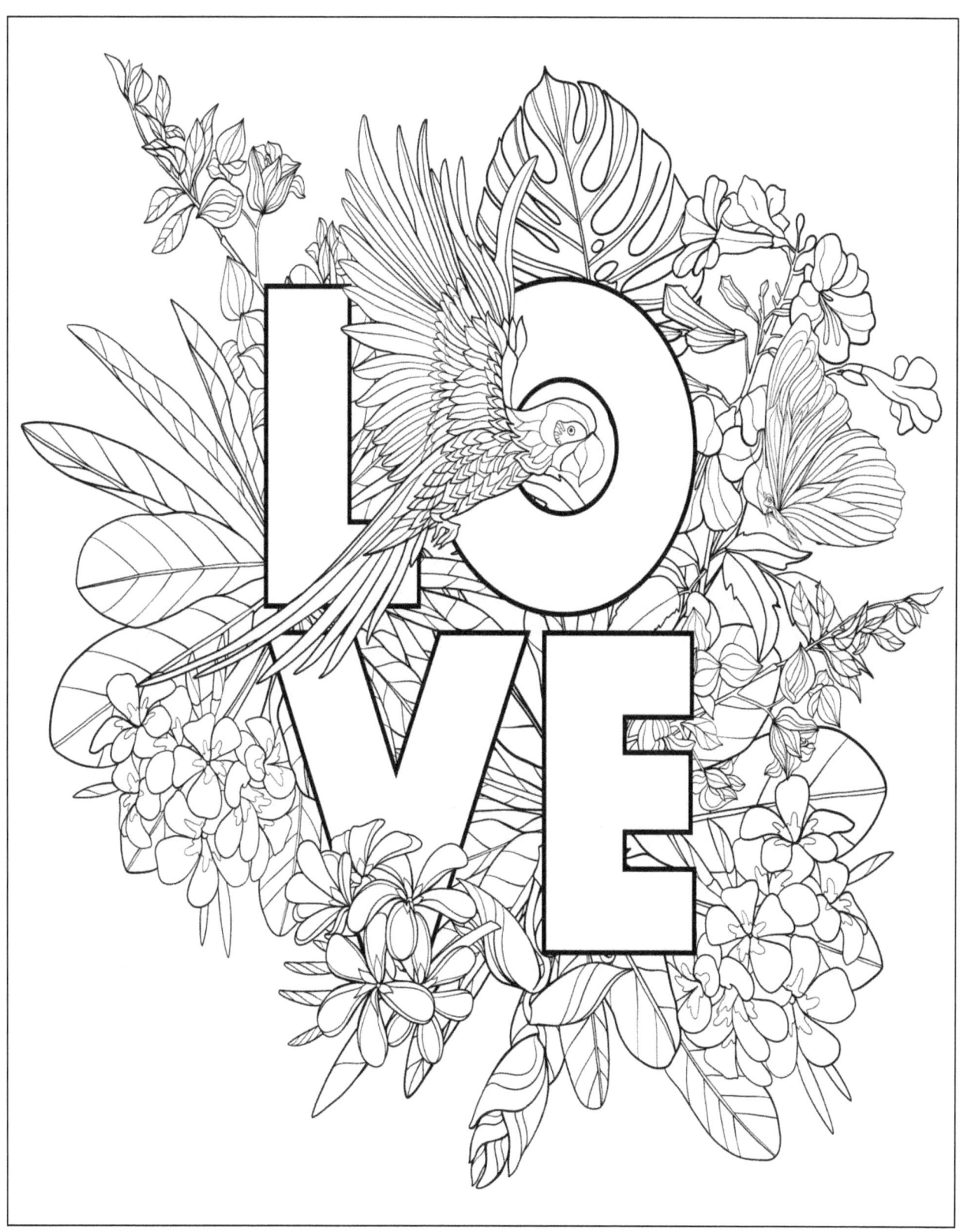

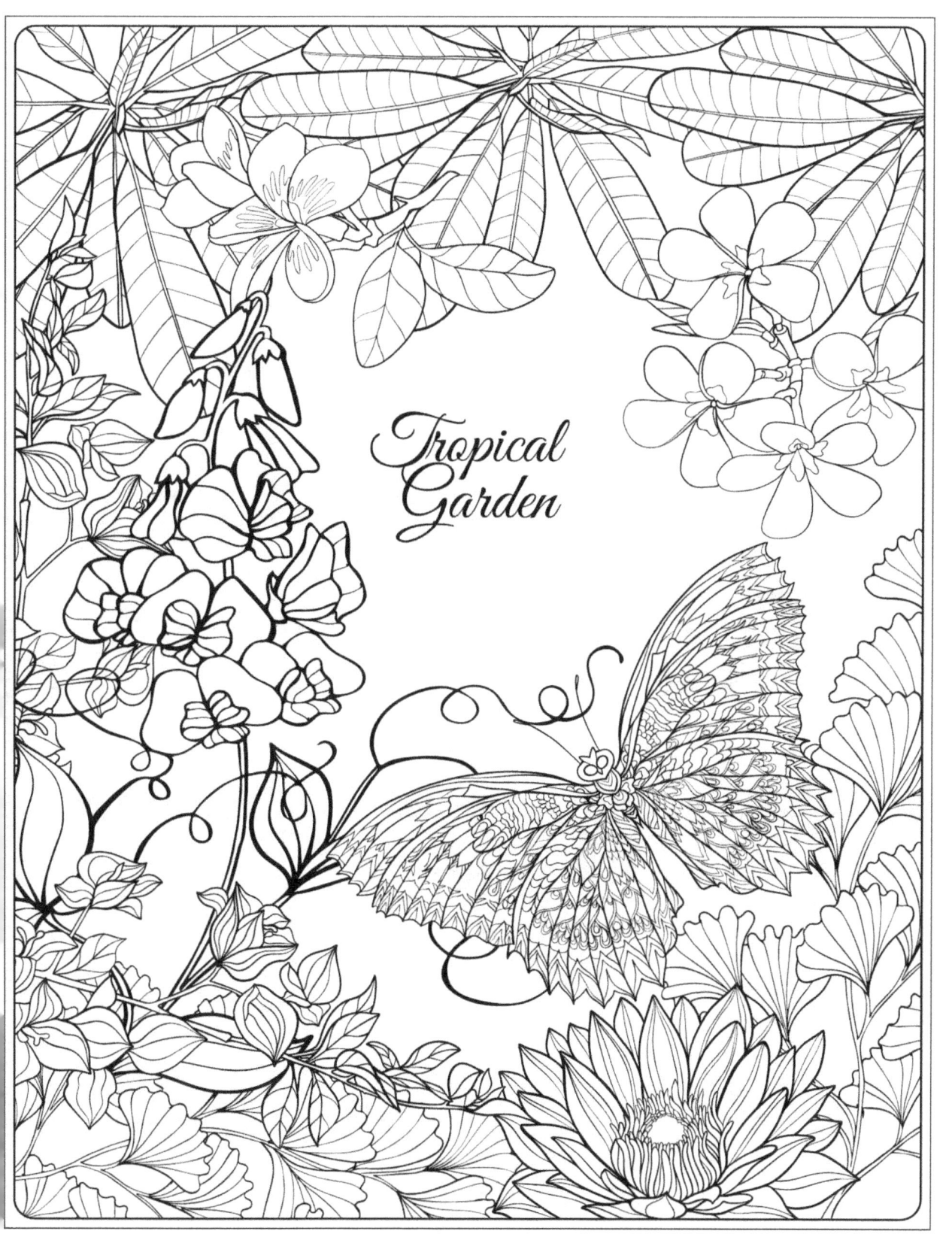

Tropical Garden

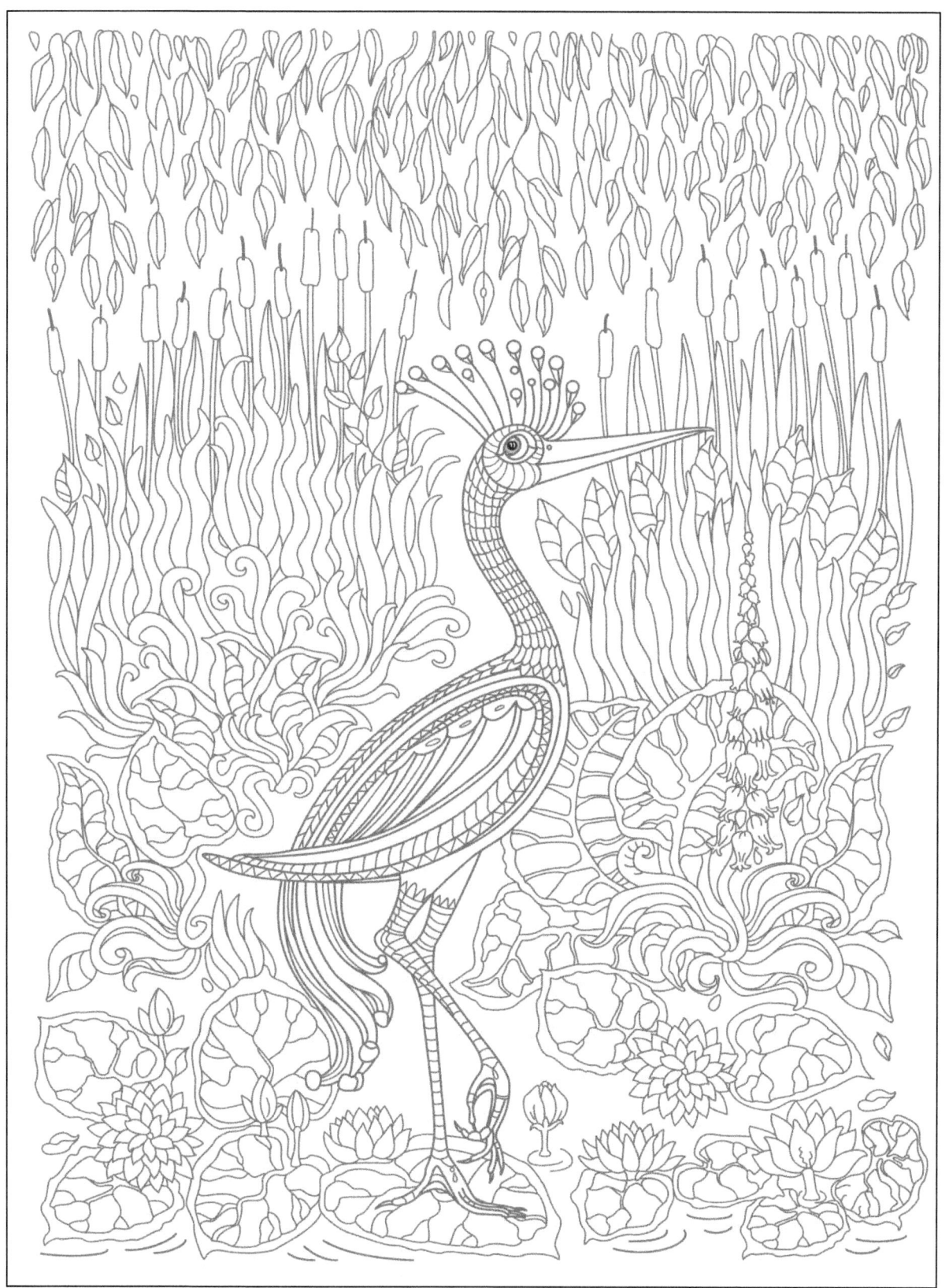

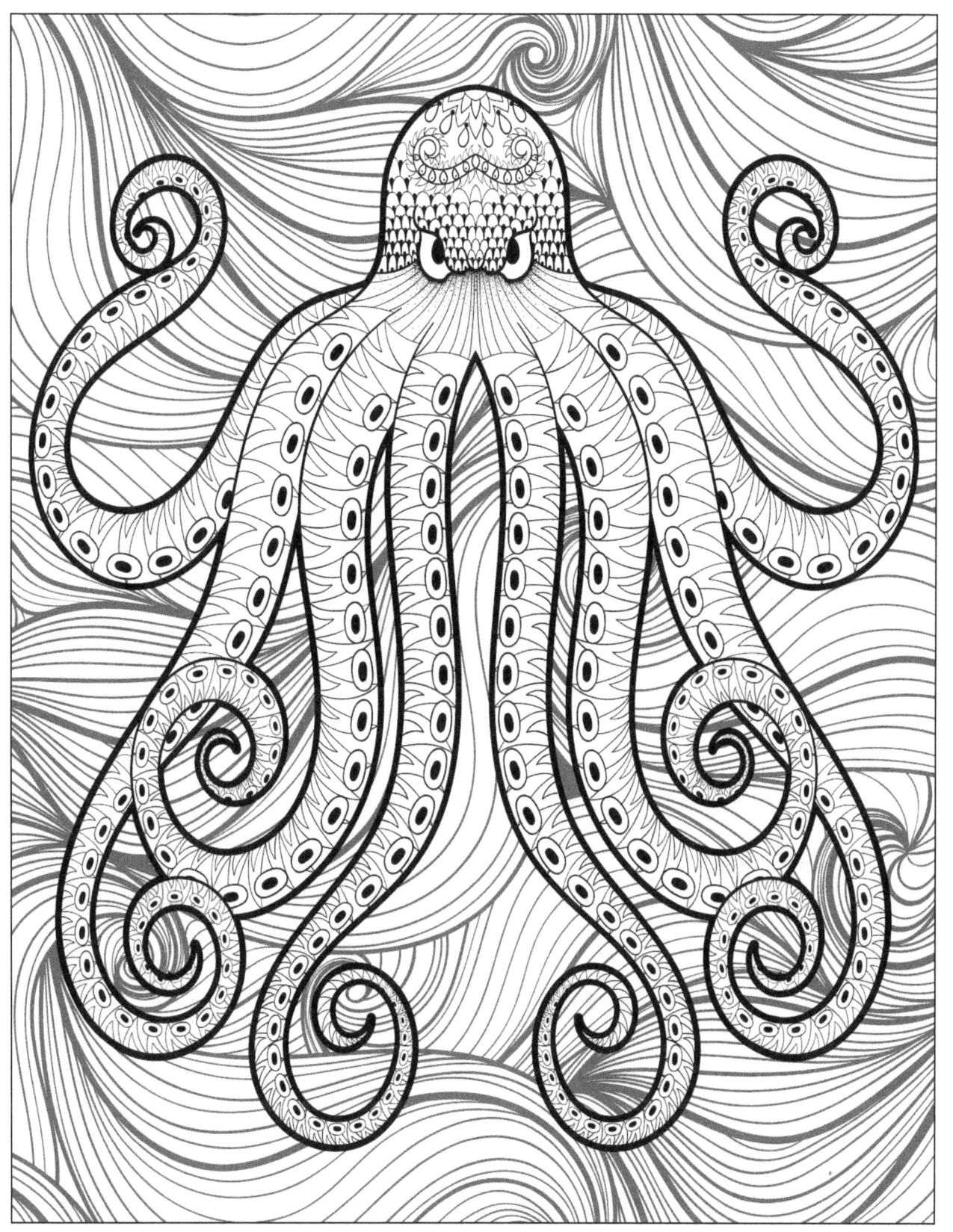

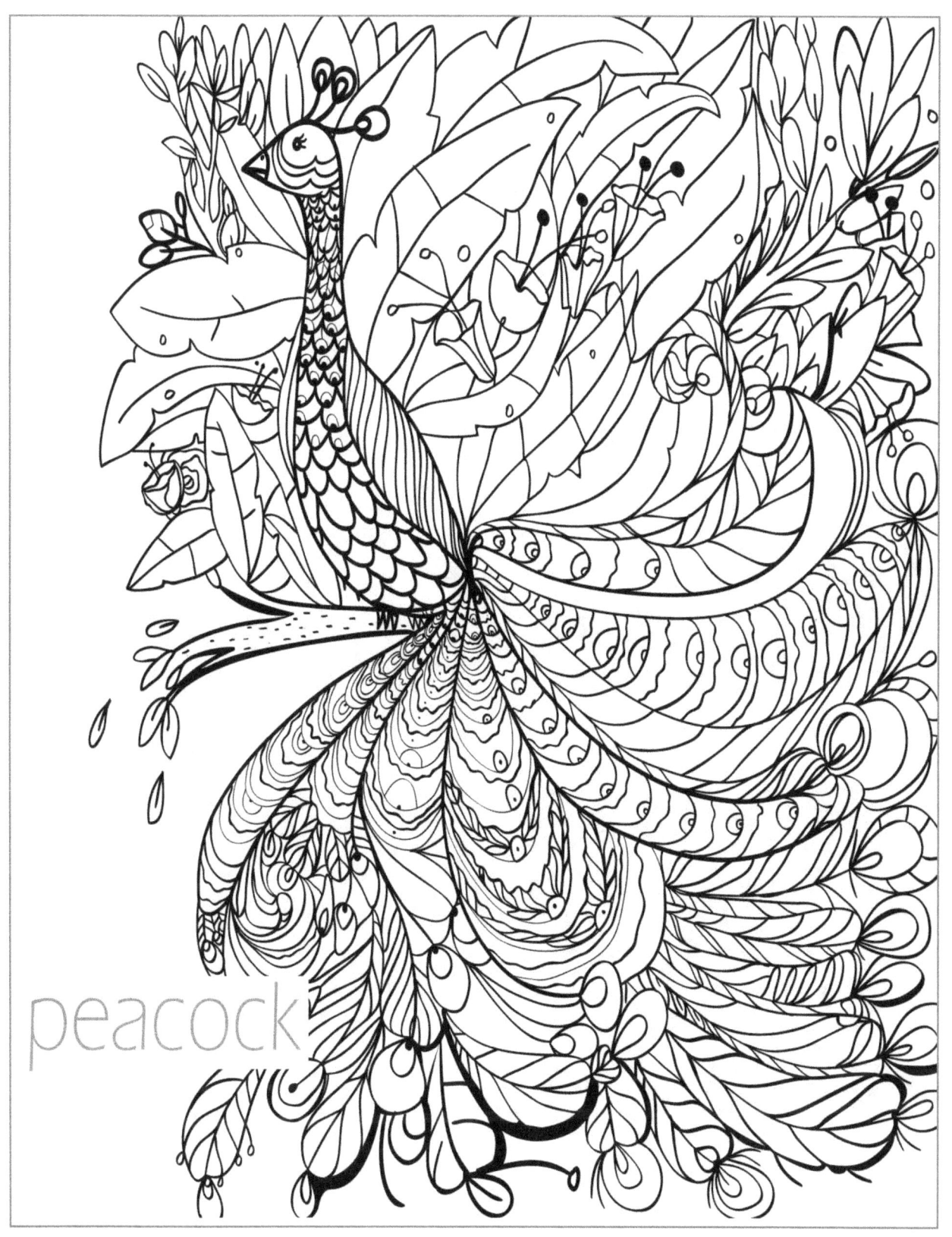

peacock

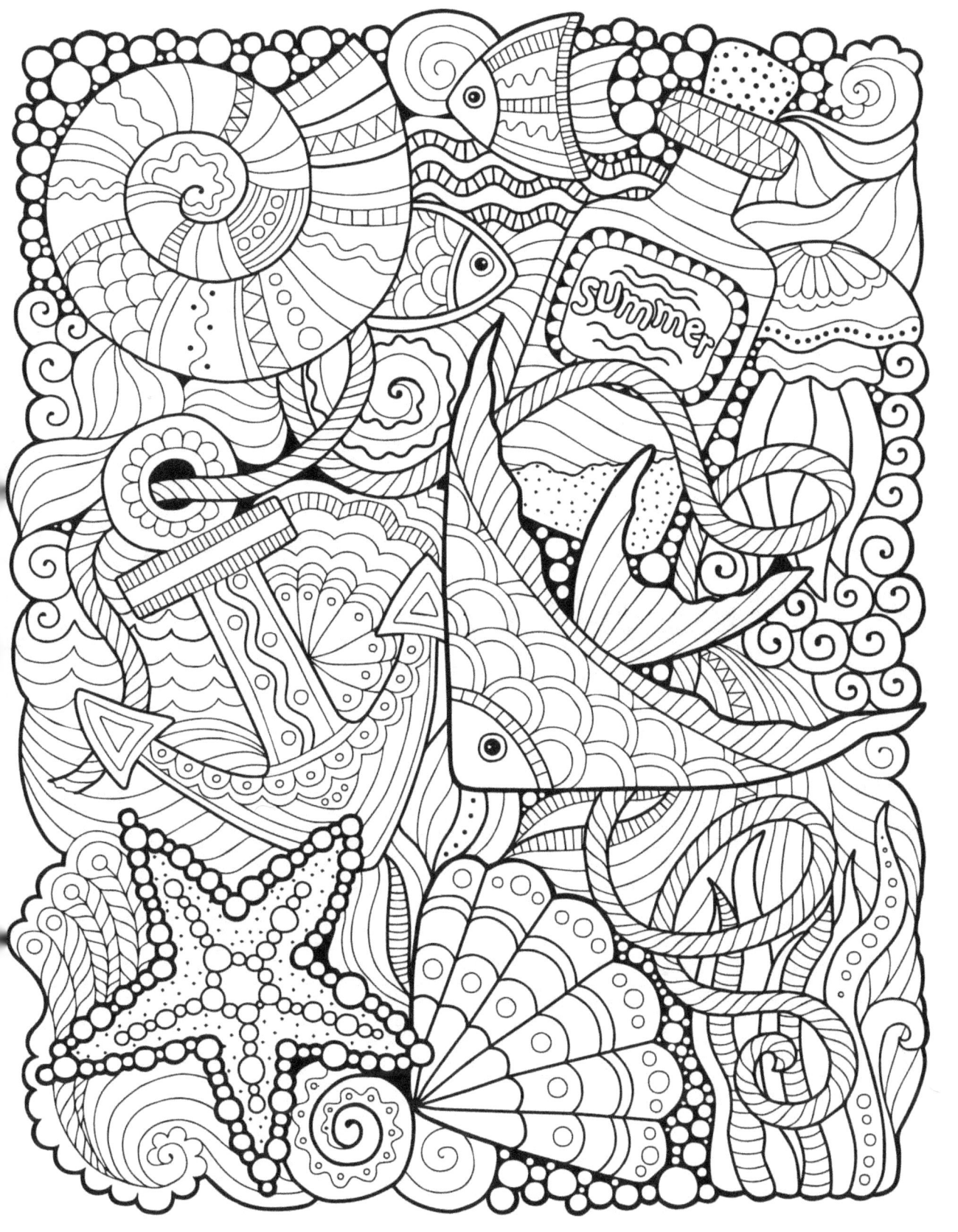

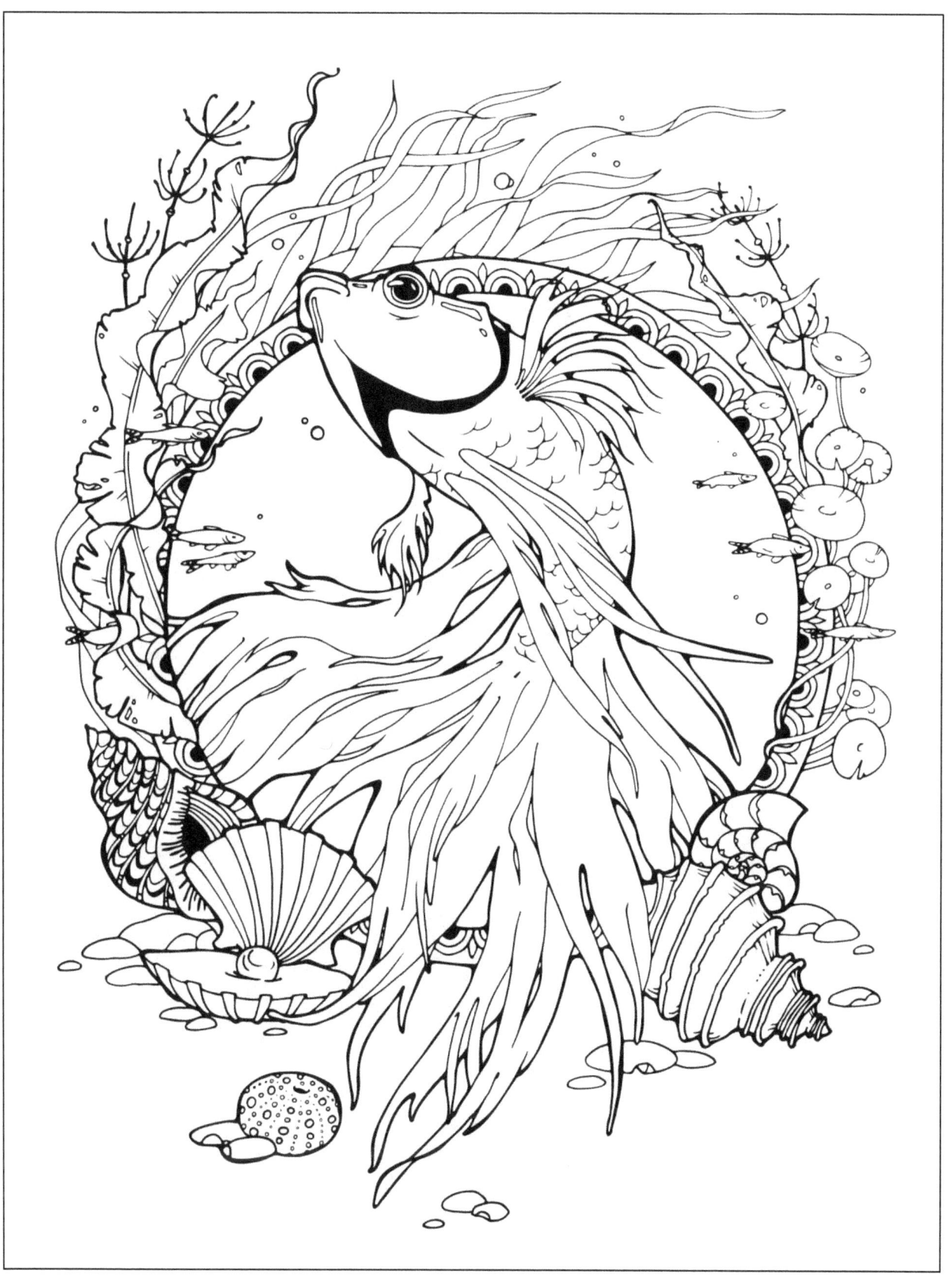

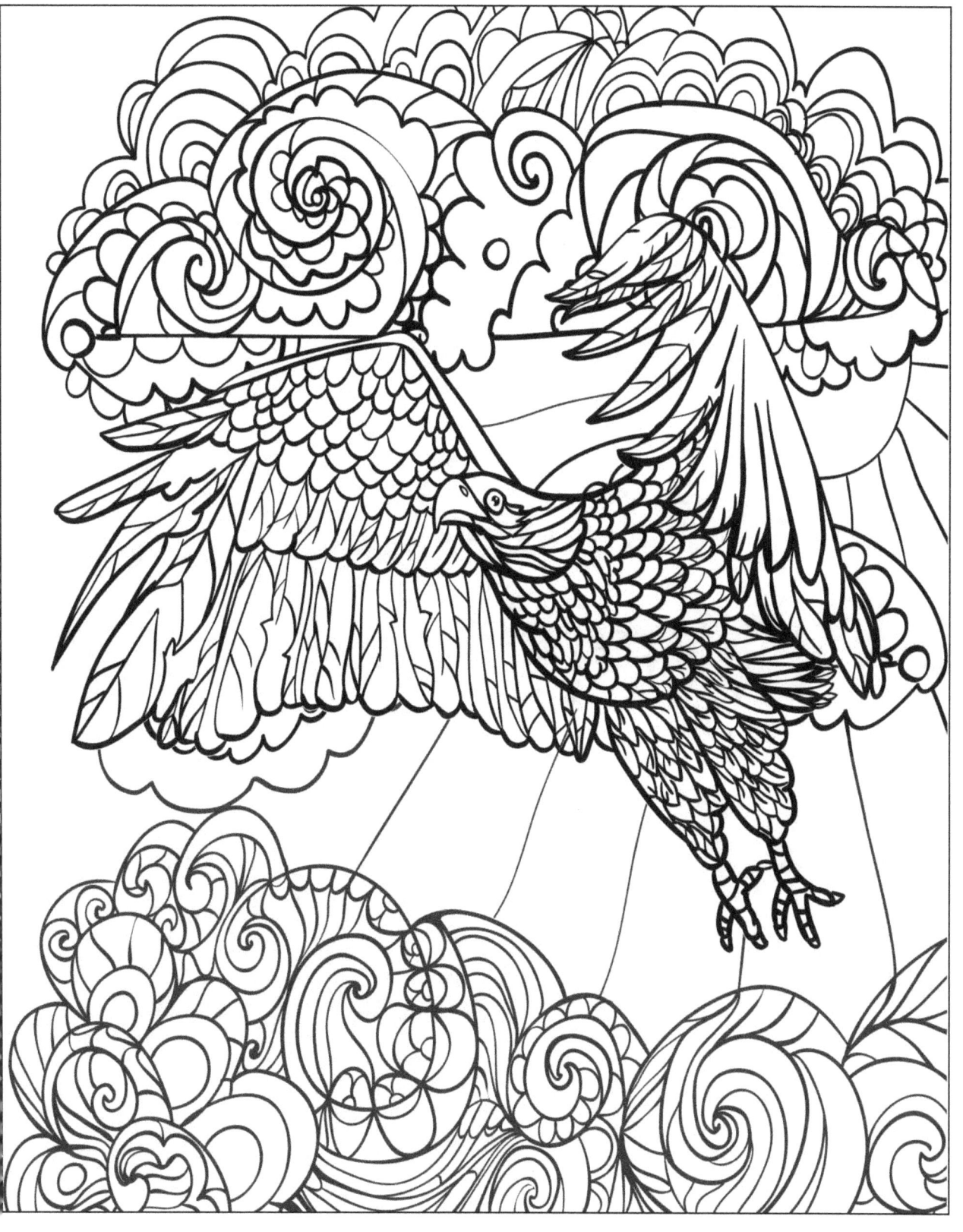

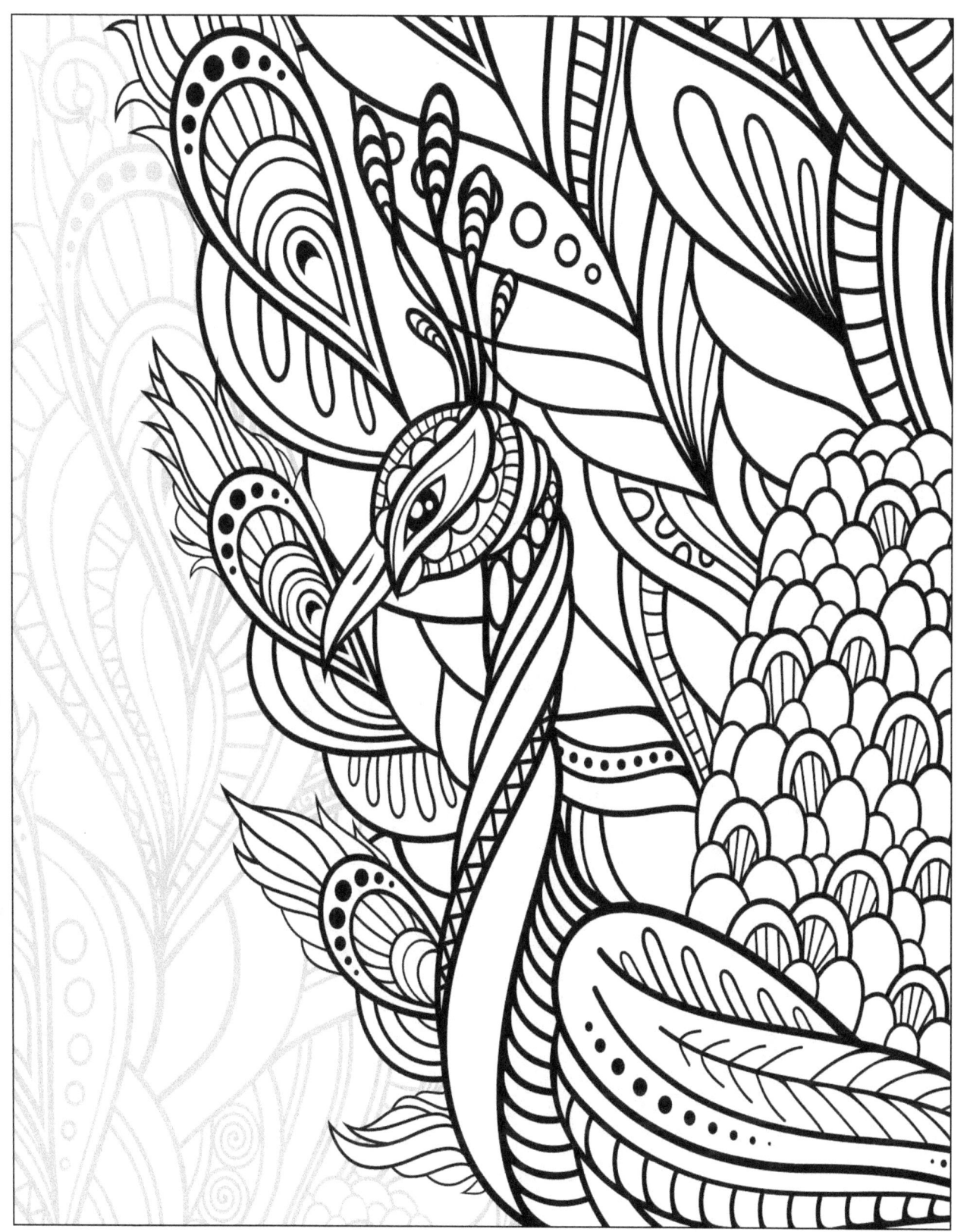

Use the following blank pages to sketch your own
designs and then color away.

Cover Image Copyright: Nadezhda Molkentin/shutterstock
Page1   Copyright: Nadezhda Molkentin/shutterstock
Page3   Copyright:handiniatmodiwiryo/shutterstock
Page5   Copyright: ImHope/shutterstock
Page7   Copyright: Nadezhda Molkentin/shutterstock
Page9   Copyright: BigBoy/shutterstock
Page11   Copyright: BigBoy/shutterstock
Page13   Copyright Kulikova Valeriya/shutterstock
Page15   Copyright: YAZZIK/shutterstock
Page17   Copyright: BigBoy/shutterstock
Page19   Copyright: ImHope/shutterstock
Page21   Copyright: Nadezhda Molkentin/shutterstock
Page23   Copyright: YAZZIK/shutterstock
Page25   Copyright: ImHope/shutterstock
Page27   Copyright: Ramunas M/shutterstock
Page29   Copyright:ImHope/shutterstock
Page31   Copyright: Helen Lane/shutterstock
Page33   Copyright: Ramunas M/shutterstock
Page35   Copyright: YAZZIK/shutterstock
Page37   Copyright: Ramunas M/shutterstock
Page39   Copyright: YAZZIK/shutterstock
Page41   Copyright: Svitlana Samokhina/shutterstock
Page43   Copyright: ImHope/shutterstock
Page45   Copyright: Helen Lane/shutterstock
Page47   Copyright: Catherine Glazkova/shutterstock
Page49   Copyright: photo-nuke/shutterstock
Page51   Copyright: Helen Lane/shutterstock
Page53   Copyright: STRYHELSKAYA VOLHA/shutterstock
Page55   Copyright: STRYHELSKAYA VOLHA/shutterstock
Page57   Copyright: Helen Lane/shutterstock
Page59   Copyright: Helen Lane/shutterstock
Page61   Copyright: L. Kramer/shutterstock
Page63   Copyright: panki/shutterstock
Page65   Copyright: STRYHELSKAYA VOLHA/shutterstock
Page67   Copyright: Toporovska Nataliia/shutterstock
Page69   Copyright Kulikova Valeriya/shutterstock
Page71   Copyright: STRYHELSKAYA VOLHA/shutterstock
Page73   Copyright: Helena Krivoruchko/shutterstock

Thank you for purchasing this amazing Coloring Book of Tropical Dreams artwork.

*If you enjoyed this book, please leave a **positive review.** If you like FREE things just email me for FREE offers and designs.*

EastonEGray@gmail.com

Please look for our new collections being released in the near future.

Peaceful moments always,
Blue Diamonds Coloring